WHY WE COOPERATE

WHY WE COOPERATE

Michael Tomasello

Based on the 2008 Tanner Lectures on
Human Values at Stanford

A Boston Review Book

THE MIT PRESS Cambridge, Mass. London, England

MIT Press books may be purchased at special quantity
discounts for business or sales promotional use. For
information, please e-mail special_sales@mitpress.mit.edu or
write to Special Sales Department, The MIT Press,
55 Hayward Street, Cambridge, MA 02142.

This book was set in Adobe Garamond by *Boston Review*
and was printed and bound in the United States of America.

Library of Congress Cataloging-in-Publication Data
Tomasello, Michael.
  Why we cooperate : based on the 2008 Tanner lectures on
human values at Stanford University / Michael Tomasello.
      p. cm.
  Includes bibliographical references.
  ISBN 978-0-262-01359-8 (hardcover : alk. paper)
  1. Helping behavior. 2. Altruism. 3. Cooperativeness. 4.
Social norms. I. Title.
  HM1146.T66 2009
  158'.3—dc22

                                    2009019631

10   9   8   7   6   5   4   3

yours

CONTENTS

INTRODUCTION

Individuals of many animal species exploit the experience and hard work of others by learning things from them socially. When individuals socially learn to the degree that different populations of a species develop different ways of doing things, biologists now speak of culture. In this very broad perspective, many animal species live in culturally distinct groups, including a variety of species of birds, marine mammals, and primates.

Humans, of course, are the paradigmatic cultural species. Unlike their nearest great-ape relatives, who all live in Africa or Asia in the general vicinity of the equator, humans have spread out all over the globe.

Everywhere they go, they invent new artifacts and behavioral practices for dealing with the exigencies of the local environment. In the Arctic, indigenous populations build igloos and hunt whales in kayaks, whereas in the Tropics they build straw huts and hunt terrestrial mammals with bows and arrows. For humans such artifacts and behavioral practices are not niceties but necessities. Few humans could survive in either the tundra or a tropical rainforest in the absence of a cultural group possessed of relevant, preexisting artifacts and behavioral practices. In terms of the number of things an individual human must socially learn (including linguistic conventions in order to communicate), human culture, as compared with that of other animal species, is quantitatively unique.

But there are two clearly observable characteristics of human culture that mark it as qualitatively unique as well. The first is what has been called cumulative cultural evolution. Human artifacts and behavioral practices often become more complex over time (they have a "history"). An individual invents an artifact or way of doing things that is adequate to the task, and others quickly learn it. But then if another individual makes some improvement, everyone, including developing children, tends to learn the new and improved version. This produces a kind of cultural ratchet, as each version of the practice stays solidly in the group's repertoire until someone comes up with something even newer and more improved.[1] This means that just as individual humans biologically inherit genes that have been adaptive in the past, they also culturally inherit artifacts and behavioral practices that represent something like the collective wisdom of their forebears.[2] To date, no animal species other than humans has been observed to have cultural behaviors that accumulate modifications and so ratchet up in complexity over time.

The second clearly observable feature of human culture that marks it as unique is the creation of social institutions. Social institutions are sets of behavioral practices governed by various kinds of mutually recognized norms and rules. For example, all human cultures engage in mating and marriage in the context of their own rules. If one violates these rules, one is sanctioned in some way, perhaps even ostracized totally. As a part of the process, humans actually create new culturally defined entities, for example, husbands and wives (and parents), who have culturally defined rights and obligations (the philosopher John Searle refers to this process as the creation of new "status functions"[3]). As a different example, all human cultures have rules and norms for sharing or possibly trading food and other valuable objects. In the process of exchange, some objects may be accorded the cultural status of money (e.g., specially marked paper), which gives them a certain, culturally backed role. Other sets of rules and norms create leaders of the group, such as chiefs and presidents, who have special rights and obligations to make decisions, or even create new rules, for the group. As for the cultural ratchet, so for social institutions: no animal species other than humans has been observed to have anything even vaguely resembling the latter.

Underlying these two singular characteristics of human culture—cumulative artifacts and social institutions—are a set of species-unique skills and motivations for cooperation. This seems especially obvious in the case of social institutions. Social institutions represent cooperatively organized and agreed-upon ways of interacting, including rules of enforcement for noncooperators. Status functions represent cooperative agreements that such entities as husbands, parents, money, and chiefs exist, and have the rights and obligations that they do. Drawing on the work of philosophers of action such as Michael Bratman, Margaret Gilbert, Searle, and Raimo Tuomela,[4] we may refer to the underlying psychological processes that make these unique forms of cooperation possible as "shared intentionality." Shared intentionality involves, most basically, the ability to create with others joint intentions and joint commitments in cooperative endeavors. These joint intentions and commitments are structured by processes of joint attention and mutual knowledge, all underlain by the cooperative motives to help and to share with others.[5]

Although less obvious, humans' ultra-cooperative tendencies also play a crucial role in the cultural ratchet. It is true that the most basic process involved is imitative learning (which humans seem to employ with great fidelity of transmission), and imitative learning is not inherently cooperative but rather exploitive. But, in addition, two fundamentally cooperative processes are critical for the human cultural ratchet as well.

First, humans actively teach one another things, and they do not reserve their lessons for kin. Teaching is a form of altruism, founded on a motive to help, in which individuals donate information to others for their use. Although a few nonhuman species engage in something like teaching (mostly for single behaviors and with offspring), there are no systematic, replicated reports of active instruction in nonhuman primates.

Second, humans also have a tendency to imitate others in the group simply in order to be like them, that is, to conform (perhaps as an indicator of group identity). Moreover, they sometimes even invoke co-operatively agreed-upon social norms of conformity on others in the group, and their appeals to conformity are backed by various potential punishments or sanctions for those who resist. To our knowledge, no other primates collectively create and enforce group norms of conformity. Both teaching and norms of conformity contribute to cumulative culture by conserving innovations in the group until some further innovation comes along.

And so, whereas the "cultures" of other animal species are based almost exclusively on imitation and other exploitive processes, the cultures of human beings are based not only on exploitation, but on fundamentally cooperative processes as well. To an unprecedented degree, *homo sapiens* are adapted for acting and thinking cooperatively in cultural groups, and indeed all of humans' most impressive cognitive achievements—from complex technologies to linguistic and mathematical symbols to intricate social institutions—are the products not of individuals acting alone, but of individuals interacting.[6] As they grow, human children are equipped to participate in this cooperative groupthink through a special kind of cultural intelligence, comprising species-unique social-cognitive skills and motivations for collaboration, communication, social learning, and other forms of shared intentionality.[7] These special skills arose from processes of cultural niche construction and gene-culture coevolution; that is to say, they arose as adaptations that enabled humans to function effectively in any one of their many different self-built cultural worlds.

To explain human cooperation and culture—to explain everything from donating to charity, to linguistic and mathematical symbols, to social institutions—multiple approaches are needed. In the contemporary arena, human cooperation and culture are studied by evolutionary biologists; experimental economists; game theorists; sociologists; cultural and biological anthropologists; cognitive, social, and evolutionary psychologists; and many others. In my own research group, we have chosen to approach these problems via comparative studies of human children and their nearest primate relatives, especially chimpanzees. The hope is that in these somewhat simpler cases we may see things more clearly than is possible in the myriad complexities of adult human behavior and societies. And, of course, child-chimpanzee comparisons may enlighten us about the origins of human cooperation in both phylogeny and ontogeny.

Our empirical research on cooperation in children and chimpanzees focuses on two basic phenomena:

(1) Altruism: one individual sacrificing in some way for another; and

(2) Collaboration: multiple individuals working together for mutual benefit.

In the first chapter, I summarize our recent research on the altruism of human children, focusing especially on its emergence in early ontogeny but also reporting some surprising observations of spontaneous helping in chimpanzees as evolutionary foundation. The basic question here is whether altruism emerges "naturally" in young children or whether, alternatively, it is somehow imparted by culture (or whether culture perhaps plays some other role). In the second chapter, I summarize our recent research on collaborative problem solving in children and chimpanzees. The basic question here is how best to characterize differences in the ways that humans and great apes engage with conspecifics—members of their same species—collaboratively. Where might these differences have come from evolutionarily, and how might they have resulted in such complex cooperative products as social norms and institutions?

I

Why We Cooperate

1

*Born (and Bred)
to Help*

A prince must learn how not to be good.
— Niccolò Machiavelli

ONE OF THE GREAT DEBATES IN WESTERN CIVI-
lization is whether humans are born cooperative and
helpful and society later corrupts them (e.g., Rousseau), or whether they are born selfish and unhelpful
and society teaches them better (e.g., Hobbes). As
with all great debates, both arguments undoubtedly
have some truth on their side. Here I defend a thesis
that mainly sides with Rousseau's take on things, but
which adds some critical complexities. I will call this
thesis, in deference to two of this book's contributors,
the *Early Spelke, Later Dweck* hypothesis. Specifically,

I will argue and present evidence that from around their first birthdays—when they first begin to walk and talk and become truly cultural beings—human children are already cooperative and helpful in many, though obviously not all, situations. And they do not learn this from adults; it comes naturally. (That is the Spelke part.) But later in ontogeny, children's relatively indiscriminate cooperativeness becomes mediated by such influences as their judgments of likely reciprocity and their concern for how others in the group judge them, which were instrumental in the evolution of humans' natural cooperativeness in the first place. And they begin to internalize many culturally specific social norms for how we do things, how one ought to do things if one is to be a member of this group. (That is the Dweck part.)

For parents who think that their child must have skipped the naturally cooperative stage, let me quickly note that we are talking here about a behavior measured in relation to other primates. All viable organisms must have a selfish streak; they must be concerned about their own survival and well-being or they will not be leaving many offspring. Human cooperativeness and helpfulness are, as it were, laid on top of this self-interested foundation.

In addition—and this will be a key complicating aspect of my account—I do not believe that human altruism is a single trait, but rather that humans are more or less altruistic in different domains of activity, each of which has its own characteristics. Felix Warneken, a fellow researcher at the Max Planck Institute, and I use an economic framework incorporating three main types of human altruism as defined by the "commodity" involved: goods, services, and information.[1] To be altruistic with respect to goods such as food is to be generous, to engage in sharing; to be altruistic with respect to services such as fetching an out-of-reach object for someone is to be helpful; and to share information and attitudes altruistically with others (including gossip) is to be informative. It is important to distinguish among these three types of altruism because the costs and benefits of each are different, and they may have different evolutionary histories.

So let us step through the empirical data available as to whether and in what ways young human children and their nearest primate relatives tend toward each of these three types of altruism.

Helping

The basic phenomenon is simple. Infants of fourteen and eighteen months of age confront an unrelated adult they have met just moments previously. The adult has a trivial problem, and the infants help him solve it—everything from fetching out-of-reach objects to opening cabinet doors when the adult's hands are full. In one study, of the 24 eighteen-month-old infants tested, 22 helped at least once, and they did so basically immediately.[2]

Each of these situations has a corresponding control condition. For example, instead of dropping his clothespin accidentally, the adult throws it down on purpose. Or instead of bumping into the cabinet with his hands full, he bumps into the cabinet while trying to do something else. In these cases the infants do nothing, showing that they do not just like fetching clothespins and opening cabinets in general.

The ways in which infants help are also remarkably varied. In the study, they helped the adult solve four different kinds of problems: fetching out-of-reach objects, removing obstacles, correcting an adult's mistake, and choosing the correct behavioral means for a task. All of the scenarios were very likely novel, at least in their particulars, for the infants. To help others flexibly in these ways, infants need, first, to be able to perceive others' goals in a variety of situations, and second, to have the altruistic motive to help them.

There are five reasons to believe that helping others with simple physical problems such as these is a naturally emerging human behavior. The first is the relatively early onset of the behavior: fourteen to eighteen months of age, before most parents have seriously started to expect their children, much less to train them, to behave pro-socially. But this is a debatable point, as infants have certainly seen adults helping others during the first year of life.

The second reason is that parental rewards and encouragement do not seem to increase infants' helping behavior. We gave one-year-olds a reward every time they helped, and on each new trial the adult had a reward visibly in his hand, but neither inducement affected helping.[3] In an ongoing study, Warneken and I gave infants an opportunity to help either on their own or when their mother was in the room and verbally encouraging them to help. Parents take heed: the parental encouragement did not affect the infants' behavior at all; they helped the same amount with or without it. It is noteworthy that in both of these studies the infants were so inclined to help in general that to keep the overall level of helping down—so that we could potentially see differences between conditions—we had to provide a distracter activity in which they were engaged when the opportunity to help arose. Nevertheless, in the vast majority of cases, they pulled themselves away from this fun activity—they paid a cost—in order to help the struggling adult.

But the situation with rewards is even more interesting. In a recent multiphase study,[4] Warneken and I gave twenty-month-olds various opportunities to help. Some of the children were given a concrete reward every time they helped: a small toy that they could use to create an exciting effect, which they loved. Other children were given no reward at all, not even a smile or a thank you from the adult who simply accepted the help with no reaction whatsoever. Most children helped on five occasions, and those who did participated in the second phase, in which the infants had the opportunity to help several times again. This time, however, there would be no reaction from the adult in any of the cases. The results were remarkable. The children who had been rewarded five times in the first phase actually helped *less* during the second phase than those who had not been rewarded.

This "overjustification effect" has been documented by the Stanford psychologist Mark Lepper and others in many domains of activity and is thought to signal that a behavior is intrinsically motivating. In the case of an intrinsically rewarding activity, external rewards undermine this intrinsic motivation—they externalize it to the reward. A behavior that was already driven by external rewards should not be affected by further rewards in this way. So not only do concrete rewards not stimulate children's helping, they may even subvert it.

The third reason to believe that infants are not helping just for rewards or in order to please parents is that chimpanzees engage in the same behavior. Warneken and I administered the battery of ten tasks from our original study to three human-raised chimpanzees. Although they did not help in the other tasks, they did help humans to fetch out-of-reach objects (and not in the control condition).[5]

We realize that there may be many reasons that human-raised chimpanzees would help the human—who, after all, controls their world—and so in another study we gave mother-raised chimpanzees the opportunity to help one another. In the study, one chimpanzee watched while another struggled to open a door to a room. The observing ape knew from previous experience that the door could be opened by removing a pin. Surprisingly, observers removed the pin and helped their group-mate gain access to the room. And there was no evidence that they expected any reward. They did not do this in two control conditions in which the group-mate was not attempting to gain access in this same way.[6] The point for current purposes is that if our nearest primate relatives—including ones whose previous contact with humans was minimal—engage in helping behavior similar to our own, there is evidence that humans' helping behavior is not created by a human-like cultural environment.

The fourth reason I will mention only briefly because the data have not been fully analyzed. A new study found that children in more traditional cultures—in which parents typically allow their children to develop with much less adult intervention—help in basically the same situations, and at basically the same ages, as the Western, middle-class children that we have studied.[7]

Fifth, and finally, a recent study has shown that young children's helping behavior is mediated by empathetic concern. Eighteen and 24-month-old infants looked on as one adult grabbed the drawing that another adult had just been working on and deliberately tore it up. As soon as this happened, infants looked to the victim (who expressed no emotion) with a facial expression that could be coded blindly and reliably as "concerned." That is, they did this more than in a control condition in which the vandal took a blank piece of paper from in front of the other adult and tore it up. In a related condition, an adult, either as victim or control, was stripped of a toy. Then, most important for current purposes, children from both conditions were given an opportunity to help the victim or the control adult. The result was that the children helped the victim more often than they helped the adult from the control condition. Significantly, the infants who displayed more concerned looks to the victim as her drawing was being torn up had a greater tendency to help her.[8] This suggests that infants' naturally occurring empathetic or sympathetic responses to the victim's plight affected their tendency to help. It is this "concern" then, we would argue, and not external rewards, that motivates young children's helping.

For these five reasons—early emergence, immunity from encouragement and undermining by rewards, deep evolutionary roots in great apes, cross-cultural robustness, and foundation in natural sympathetic emotions—we believe that children's early helping is not a behavior created by culture and/or parental socialization practices. Rather, it is an outward expression of children's natural inclination to sympathize with others in strife. Research in other laboratories is consistent with this conclusion: even infants below one year of age distinguish helpful from unhelpful agents.[9]

Informing

Although both chimpanzees and young human children help others in some situations, there is one special form of helping in which only children engage: providing needed information. Importantly, this is not dependent on language. Human infants inform others from as early as twelve months of age, pre-linguistically, by pointing. Chimpanzees and other apes do not point for one another at all, and, I will argue, they do not use any other means of communication to helpfully inform one another of things either.

Researchers set up a situation in which twelve-month-old, pre-linguistic infants watched while an adult engaged in some adult-centered task such as stapling papers. The adult also manipulated another object during the same period of time. Then she left the room, and another adult came in and moved the two objects to some shelves. The original adult then came back in, papers in hand, ready to continue stapling. But there was no stapler on her table, as she searched for it gesturing quizzically but not talking at all. As in the instrumental helping studies, the infants perceived the adult's problem and were motivated to help her, which most of them did by pointing to the location of the sought-for stapler. The children were far less likely to point at the other object, which had been handled an equal amount. The infants did not want the stapler for themselves. They did not engage in the usual demanding behavior—whining, reaching, and so forth—after the adult grasped the stapler. Once she had it in her hand, the children stopped pointing and were satisfied.[10] In follow-up studies, the researchers also ruled out that infants simply wanted to see the stapling activity reinstated.[11]

While infants consistently demonstrate understanding of informative pointing, the same is not true of apes. Apes do not point for one another, and when they do point for humans, they do so mainly to get humans to fetch food for them.[12] Indeed, in all observed cases of apes pointing for humans, the motive is directive (imperative). Also, apes who have learned some kind of human-centered communication use it to communicate only with humans, not with one another, and they do so almost exclusively for directive purposes. Some years ago, my colleague Josep Call and I observed that if a human needed a tool to open a box that contained food for the ape, the ape would point to the location of the tool for the human.[13] One could interpret this as informing the human, but it is also possible that the ape is imperatively ordering the human to "get the tool." A recent study directly compared apes and human children as they pointed for tools in a situation like this one, except that in one condition the tool was used by the human to fetch something for the ape, whereas in another condition the tool was used by the human to fetch something for herself.[14] The researchers used an "ABA" design. In the first and third sessions, ape and child subjects pointed to a tool the adult human used to fetch something for them. But in the middle session, they were supposed to point to a tool the adult human used to fetch something for herself (with no reward for the subject). The main finding was that the apes only pointed reliably when they themselves would get something in the end, which is consistent with the interpretation that their pointing is really a directive ("get the tool"). The infants, on the other hand, pointed equally often in both cases. Interestingly, some infants appeared upset when the adult wanted the tool in order to fetch a reward for herself. Nevertheless, they pointed to the tool for her when she looked around, puzzled; they could not help but be informative.

Perhaps surprisingly, apes do not even comprehend pointing when it is used in an informative manner. Apes follow gaze and pointing direction to visible targets, but they do not seem to grasp an informative communicative intent. Thus, in many different studies we have found that when apes are searching for hidden food, and a human points to a cup to inform them of its location, the apes do not understand; they do not ask themselves why the pointer wanted them to attend to the cup, they do not seek relevance.[15] This makes perfect ape sense because in their everyday lives apes do not experience someone pointing out food for them helpfully—they compete with others for food—so they do not assume an altruistic intent. Human infants, on the other hand, understand informative pointing and make the appropriate relevance inference in such situations pre-linguistically, at twelve to fourteen months of age.[16] Confronted with pointing, infants appear to ask themselves, "why does *she* think that my attending to that cup will be helpful or relevant for *me*?" This self-question is based on something like the philosopher Paul Grice's principle of cooperation: others are trying to be helpful by informing me of things relevant not to themselves but to their interlocutors. Chimpanzees do not operate with anything like a Gricean principle of cooperation—fittingly, in their natural worlds—and thus they have no basis for making the appropriate relevance inference.

But what about ape alarm calls and food calls? Are they not generated by an informative intent? In a word, no. When they spy a predator, nonhuman primates give their alarm calls even if all of the other members of the group are right there looking at the predator and screaming themselves; they give food calls when they discover a rich source of food, even if the whole group is with them already. Their goal in such situations cannot be to inform others, as everyone is clearly already in the know. Whatever they are doing, it is for their own, or their kin's, direct benefit. (One may speculate that with alarm calls they are alerting the predator that he has been spotted or recruiting others to mob the predator, and with food calls they are ensuring that they have company to protect against predators while they eat.) Apes do not, in either gesture or vocalizations, intend to inform one another of things helpfully.[17]

Human infants, on the other hand, not only inform others of things helpfully and accurately interpret informative intentions directed at them, they even understand imperatives in a cooperative fashion. Thus, most human imperatives are not commands, e.g., "get me water," but rather something more indirect, such as "I'd like some water," which is just a statement of desire. I can get water by informing others of my desire because they are so cooperative that simply knowing my desire leads them automatically to want to fulfill it. In a recent study, a researcher asked twenty-month-old infants to fetch her "the battery," with one battery on the table right in front of her and the other on a table across the room. If the children viewed the researcher's statement as a command to fetch, pure and simple, then either battery would fulfill the directive equally well. But if they viewed it as a cooperative request for help, then the logic of helping specifies that she would only be asking for help doing something that she could not more easily do for herself. So she would likely be asking for the battery across the room. And that is exactly what the young children assumed, showing that for them, the imperative mode can sometimes be a request for help based on the cooperative logic of helping.[18]

Thus, the comparison between children and apes is different in the case of informing. When it comes to informing, as opposed to instrumental helping, humans do some things cooperatively that apes seemingly do not do at all. This suggests that altruism is not a general trait, but rather that altruistic motives may arise in some domains of activity but not in others. In the next chapter I will try to provide an evolutionary explanation for why only humans help others by providing needed information. In terms of ontogeny, it seems hard to imagine that these twelve-month-old infants are providing information helpfully because they have been rewarded or encouraged to do so; sharing information freely seems to come naturally even to very young children. Of course children soon learn to lie also, but that comes only some years later and presupposes preexisting cooperation and trust. If people did not have a tendency to trust one another's helpfulness, lying could never get off the ground.

Sharing

Virtually all experts agree that apes are not very altruistic in the sharing of resources such as food. Sharing valuable resources is obviously a more difficult proposition than simply helping humans by expending a few ergs of energy fetching or pointing to things for them. And if our plane crashes in the Andes, and I have one granola bar left in my pocket, I, a human, am not likely to be so generous with it either. Nevertheless, in more-or-less direct comparisons in two experimental settings, human children were more generous with food and valued objects than were our great-ape relatives.

First, two similar studies—one at our laboratory and one at UCLA—found that chimpanzees do not seem to care at all about the food others may or may not be receiving. In one version, the chimpanzee subject was faced with the choice of pulling in one of two boards, on each of which were two reward trays: one tray accessible to the subject and one tray accessible to another individual in an adjoining cage. In the simplest situation, one of the boards contained one piece of food for the subject and none for the partner, whereas the other board contained one piece of food for each. Thus, the energy that a subject needed to expend was identical in the two cases, and the reward for the subject (one piece of food) was also unchanged. The question was whether the chimpanzees would pull the board that would also deliver some food to the partner—at absolutely no cost to themselves. The answer in both studies is that they did not. Nor did they systematically try to prevent the other from getting food by always pulling the one that only had food for them. They pulled indiscriminately, as they seemed to be focused only on the possibility of acquiring food for themselves. To ensure that they knew what food was going to the other cage, the study included a control condition in which the other cage was empty and the door to it was open so that the pulling chimp could quickly get the food designated for the other cage. In this case they most often pulled the board with pieces of food for both cages.[19] Researchers have recently shown that both 25-month olds and school-age children in a very similar paradigm select the equitable option more often than the selfish option.[20]

One might naturally puzzle over the fact that in the Warneken helping studies, chimpanzees seem to help others attain their instrumental goals, yet in the pulling study they do not help the other get food even when doing so costs them nothing. We are currently working on a study to help resolve this puzzle, but for the moment our best speculation is that in the food-pulling experimental paradigm, the chimpanzees are focused on getting food for themselves—what happens to the other is irrelevant—whereas in the various helping paradigms, the chimpanzees are not in a position to get food for themselves at all, so their own foraging needs and competitive strategies do not predominate.

In a second experimental paradigm, we can see the effects of food competition among chimpanzees quite directly. Led by Alicia Melis, researchers at the Max Planck Institute presented chimpanzees with a food-laden board with two cords attached. The board could be reeled in only with the cooperation of both subjects. In previous studies, chimpanzees had performed this task poorly. But in those studies, the food was always clumped in the middle of the board, ensuring that sharing became a problem. The team replicated this effect, but in addition they presented the chimpanzees with a condition in which the food was already divided—some on one end of the board for one partner and some on the other end for the other partner. This time they were far more adept collaborators. It seems that the chimpanzees had previously performed badly not because they could not handle the task cognitively, but rather because they were already thinking of the fight at the end as they tried to work together.[21] Recently, Warneken and his team have done the same study with young children, and the children do not really care whether the food is pre-divided. It is not that the children always divide the food equally. Sometimes one individual will take more than her share, but then the partner challenges her to square things up, which she almost always does. This means that both partners are still ready to try again on the next trial, trusting that they will be able to work it out. Chimpanzees do not have this trust.

But what about in more natural settings? There have been some recent studies of male chimpanzees in the wild sharing food with potential coalition and mating partners, but this is almost certainly barter, not generosity.[22] If chimpanzees are presented with a low-quality food such as branches of leaves tied together by humans, they are tolerant of others feeding from the same branches;[23] however, the natural behavior of feeding chimpanzees is to separate themselves from others by a few meters as they eat, and to relinquish food only under direct begging or harassment. Human infants, in contrast, like giving objects to people—indeed offering objects to them—and these objects are often food. But at the same time, they can become attached to objects and stubbornly refuse to let them go. We are on shaky ground here because there are no comparative experiments—it very well could be that the key factor is that infants simply do not care about most objects or food very much—so to call them generous, would be, well, generous. Nevertheless it appears that in natural settings, even very young children give away and offer objects and food more readily than do their simian cousins.

A final, illustrative comparison between humans and apes appears in the sharing of food between mothers and their children. As foragers, chimpanzee youngsters are on their own, even somewhat in competition with their mothers. A recent study looked systematically at food sharing among three mother-infant pairs. Researchers recorded 84 attempts by the infant to get food from the mother; 50 of these were rejected. And more active transfers of food by the mothers were rare, occurring only fifteen times. Tellingly, when mothers did transfer food to their children more actively it was always—100 percent of the time—the less palatable part of the food they were eating. That is, the peeling, the husk, or the shell.[24] This is more than they would do for other adults or non-kin children, so there are clearly some maternal instincts at work here. But human mothers actively provision their infants—or buy them off with junk food—at a much more unsparing rate.

In the case of sharing resources such as food, then, human children seem to be more generous than chimpanzees. But here, again, I would emphasize that this is only a matter of degree. Starving humans are not so generous with food, either. It is just that chimpanzees act as if they were always starving.

Reciprocity and Norms

There is very little evidence in any of these three cases—helping, informing, and sharing—that the altruism children display is a result of acculturation, parental intervention, or any other form of socialization. But socialization does play a critical role, obviously, as children mature. Different individuals have different experiences, and different cultures have different values and social norms—these have an impact.

The influences of the child's social world may be divided into two broad sets. One is the child's direct social experience—interaction with others and lessons learned about how to interact with others based on their reactions and the resulting outcomes. On the positive side, children learn that in most situations being cooperative and helpful engenders cooperation and helpfulness in return, so they are encouraged in this direction. On the more cautious side, children also learn that always being cooperative and helpful may lead to others taking advantage of them.

Thus, after their initial period of a kind of indiscriminate altruism mixed with some selfishness about valuable things, young children become more discerning based on various characteristics of potential targets of their altruism. Several recent studies have shown that children begin to make these judgments about others from around three years of age. In one study, children at around this age *share* more often if the recipient was previously nice to them and is from their group.[25] Researchers in our lab found something similar with a helping measure: children of this age more often *help* those who have been helpful to others.[26] So children begin learning early in life who and who not to be nice to based on their own experiences with those people. This is perhaps not so surprising; recent observations—both in the wild and in experiments—have documented that even chimpanzees reciprocate grooming, support in fights, and access to food.[27]

The other set of social influences on children involves the values and norms of the cultural group, which the child experiences less through direct feedback from interactions with others and more through modeling, communication, and instruction. Cultures typically try to promote helpfulness and cooperation in their children through various kinds of social norms: be nice, be helpful, don't lie, share your toys. These have a positive side—people admire us if we live up to some valued social norm—but evolutionarily it is likely that the original function of norms is to threaten punishment for violators, everything from gossip about reputation to ostracism from the group to death by stoning. Children at some point become aware that they are the targets of the judgments of others who are using social norms as standards. So children attempt to influence these judgments—what the sociologist Erving Goffman called "impression management." Through this kind of vigilance is born the public self, whose reputation we all spend so much time and energy cultivating and defending.[28] Social norms represent, in some complex way, the perspective and values of the social group as a whole.

The authors of one recent and much-publicized study have claimed that some nonhuman primates (in this case, capuchin monkeys) have a normative sense of fairness.[29] In a similar study focused on chimpanzees, the researchers found that when a human gives a chimpanzee a low-quality food, such as a cucumber, she will normally accept it. But when the experimenter shows favor to a second chimpanzee, giving that ape a high-quality food such as a grape, the first chimpanzee, having seen the gifting of the grape, will reject the cucumber that she was previously prepared to accept. The authors' interpretation depends on social comparison—she got something better than I did—and a sense of fairness—this unequal distribution is not fair.[30]

But studies from three different laboratories in the case of the capuchins, and from our laboratory in the case of the chimpanzees, have all found that this is a spurious result in that it does not depend on a social comparison at all. One of the studies found that simply seeing and expecting to receive the grape makes the cucumber look less attractive to chimpanzees. No other individuals need be around.[31] There is no social comparison going on, only food comparison. So nothing related to norms of fairness is at work either.

In another study in our laboratory, we presented the ultimatum game from experimental economics to chimpanzees. In the human version of the game, a subject is given an amount of real money, say 100 euros, and is told that she should offer some to an unknown partner. This partner, who knows how much has been given to the subject, may then accept the offer, in which case both partners take their shares and go home. Or the partner may reject the offer, and no one gets anything. There are some cultural variations in how humans react, but by far the most common reaction of partners in this game is to reject low offers, less than about 30 euros. The logic of rational maximizing would say, "Take the 25 euros because, even though that guy is a jerk, 25 is better than none." But people do not do this; they reject low offers because, as subjects report, they are not fair. Proposers anticipate this, by the way, and so typically offer an even split.

By contrast, in this game chimpanzees are rational maximizers. Researchers constructed a mini-ultimatum game in which the proposer was faced with two trays with a pre-established division of food for himself and for the partner. For example, in one condition the choice was between "eight grapes for me, two for you" versus "five for each of us." The proposer then pulled the tray as far as he could, halfway, and the responder then had the choice of completing the deal by pulling the tray the rest of the way—or not, which would be a rejection. Humans typically reject as unfair an offer of "eight for me, two for you" when "five for each of us" is the alternative. But the chimpanzees did not. Chimpanzee proposers almost always made selfish offers, and responders almost always accepted anything, except zero (showing that they were not just pulling indiscriminately).[32] In this experiment as well, then, we see no evidence that chimpanzees operate with social norms of fairness.[33]

Humans, on the other hand, operate with two general types of social norms, with many hybrids: norms of cooperation (including moral norms) and norms of conformity (including constitutive rules). The vast majority of research with children has been conducted on moral norms, where children judge as "wrong" actions in which one person harms another. But children also respect conventional norms in which no harm is involved. Even preschool children understand that people often wear shorts in hot weather, but that is not because they think they are supposed to, whereas they wear coats and ties to weddings for precisely the latter reason. Dress at weddings is a social norm governed by people's expectations and attitudes, whereas dress in hot weather is not. Importantly, children do not just follow norms as they encounter them, but in new situations they actively seek out what they are supposed to do—what the social norms and rules are in the situation—so that they can behave accordingly. On their first day in a new classroom, for example, children want to know what they are supposed to do with their coats. When they learn that we hang our coats on the rack before sitting down at our desks each morning, they understand this as the way "things are done" here, and they want to do it this way too.[34]

The deep question is why children respect social norms. Where does the teacher's admonition, "Coats go here," get its force? Why might one listen when a peer says, "That's the rule"? Following Durkheim, Jean Piaget famously argued that the force emanates from two sources: (1) authority, coming from interactions with adults; and (2) reciprocity, coming from interactions with coequals. In Piaget's account, early in development, children respond only to norms based on authority, resting ultimately on adults' superior power. So these norms are not really norms at all, in a sense, as the child has not given them her independent sanction. True social norms based on reciprocity emerge in the late preschool period, as children lose their egocentrism and begin to see others and themselves as coequal autonomous agents. Norms based on reciprocity have power by virtue of a kind of social contract among peers founded on mutual respect. Thus, they are true norms.[35]

There is no doubt that authority and reciprocity play important roles in children's respect for social norms, but a recent series of studies suggests that Piaget's story is not quite right. It turns out that not only do children actively follow social norms, but from almost as early as they follow them they also participate in enforcing them. In one of the studies, three-year-old children were shown how to play a one-player game. When a puppet later entered and announced that it, too, would play the game, but then did so in a different way, most of the children objected, sometimes vociferously. The children's language when they objected demonstrated clearly that they were not just expressing their personal displeasure at a deviation. They made generic, normative declarations like, "It doesn't work like that," "One can't do that," and so forth.[36] They do not merely disapprove of the puppet playing the game differently; he is playing it improperly. This behavior is of critical importance, as it is one thing to follow a norm—perhaps to avoid the negative consequences of not following it—and it is quite another to legislate the norm when not involved oneself.

There are two noteworthy facts about this study. First, the rules or norms are not just regulative rules that act as a kind of traffic cop of social interaction; rather they are constitutive rules that actually create the game—and the game is then solitary, not cooperative, after one has learned it. This shows that children view even simple conventional norms of how a game is played not just as instrumental guides to their own effective action—actions likely to please powerful adults or garner some other reward—but as supra-individual entities that carry social force independent of such instrumental considerations. Second, in these studies we originally thought that to convey the idea that there was a right way and a wrong way to play the game, the child should watch the adult make a mistake and correct himself. But it turns out that was not necessary. The children had only to see the adult demonstrate the game—in a straightforward way with no normative judgments or language—before they jumped to normative conclusions about how the game *should* be played.

What these studies show is that even children's very earliest norms—at around three years of age—are true social norms (although there are still developments to come), and they result from something more than either the fear of authority or the promise of reciprocity. Although sensitivity to social pressures such as authority and reciprocity alone may be able to account for a child's tendency to cooperate and conform, they cannot account for the child's active enforcement of social norms. Children are not forced or even encouraged to enforce norms on others, so why do they do it? They are definitely not mimicking adults sanctioning others in our experiments, as they never see adults sanctioning either others or themselves in the context of the games. And if one posits that they are mimicking adults sanctioning others in some general way based on past experience in similar games, which is dubious at best, then we must ask why adults do it. Indeed, in many formulations, enforcing norms is an act of altruism, as the whole group benefits from my attempts to make the transgressor shape up, which only makes norm-enforcement by young children even more mysterious.

What is needed is a recognition that even young children already have some sense of shared intentionality, that is to say, that they are part of some larger "we" intentionality. I contend that without this added dimension of some kind of "we" identity and rationality, it is impossible to explain why children take it upon themselves to actively enforce social norms on others from a third-party stance, especially those norms that are not based on cooperation but rather on constitutive rules that are, in an important sense, arbitrary.[37] And, after the child sees how the game is played, it is played alone, so reciprocity cannot play a role. In these kinds of solitary, rule-based games, the only basis for normative sanctions is that "we" don't do it like that.

My proposal, therefore, is that children's respect for social norms is not due solely to their sensitivity to authority and reciprocity. From a young age, children also possess a kind of social rationality along the lines of what the philosopher Thomas Nagel proposes in *The Possibility of Altruism*, what we might call a "he is me" attitude of identification with others and a conception of the self as one among many, leading to the impersonal "view from nowhere."[38] This is especially clear in cooperative activities based on shared intentionality, about which I will have much more to say in the next chapter. In shared cooperative activities, we have a joint goal that creates an interdependence among us—indeed, creates an "us." If we are carrying a table to the bedroom, I cannot simply drop it and run off without hurting us and our goal. In shared cooperative activities, my individual rationality—I want to transport the table to the bedroom so I should do X—is transformed into a social rationality of interdependence: *we* want to transport the table to the bedroom, so I should do X and you should do Y.

These studies demonstrate that even outside of such cooperative activities, children also value conformity to the group—both their own and that of others. Initially children base such "we-ness" on identification with significant-other individuals such as parents and family and schoolmates (G. H. Mead's significant other), and only later generalize them into truly impersonal cultural norms based on identification with some type of cultural group (Mead's generalized other).[39] Young children thus become more adult-like in their understanding of social norms by coming to comprehend ever more about: (a) the "arbitrary" nature of norms, based on consensus[40]; and (b) the independence of norms from any specific individuals (their "agent-neutral" status).

The universality of social norms, and their critical role in human evolution, is apparent. All of the well-studied traditional societies incorporate powerful social norms about what one can and cannot do, even (or perhaps especially) in the most biologically relevant domains such as food and sex. Humans have developed special emotions adapted for the presence of norms, further demonstrating their critical role in the evolution of the species. Guilt and shame presuppose some kind of social norms, or at least social judgments, that people internalize and use to judge themselves (with feeling). In one interpretation guilt and shame are kinds of self-punishments that serve, first, to make it less likely that I will engage in the same transgression in the future, and second, to display to others that I indeed hew to the norm, even if I did not live up to it in this case. (In studies with adults, onlookers are much less likely to think badly of someone who causes some harm accidentally if that person immediately displays outward signs of guilt.) Guilt and shame are thus biologically based emotional reactions, which presuppose the kinds of normative (or at least punitive) social environments that humans have constructed for themselves. They are thus particularly good exemplars of the co-evolutionary process between human biology and culture.[41]

So the development of altruistic tendencies in young children is clearly shaped by socialization. They arrive at the process with a predisposition for helpfulness and cooperation. But then they learn to be selective about whom to help, inform, and share with, and they also learn to manage the impression they make on others—their public reputation and self—as a way of influencing the actions of those others toward themselves. In addition, they learn the social norms that characterize the cultural world in which they live, and they actively attempt to learn what these are and to follow them. They even begin to participate in the enforcement process by reminding others of the norms—as in our studies in which children tell others "how it is done"—and punishing themselves through guilt and shame when they do not live up to them. All of this reflects not only humans' special sensitivity to social pressure of various kinds, but also a kind of group identity and social rationality that is inherent in all activities involving a shared, "we" intentionality.

So is the devilish Hobbes or the angelic Rousseau correct? Are humans by nature kind or mean-spirited? As always in these types of all-encompassing questions, the answer is a bit of both. I have presented hopefully convincing empirical evidence that infants and young children come to culture ready to be helpful, informative, and generous in the right situations (though selfish in others, of course). But as they become independent, children must be more selective and aim their altruistic acts toward others who will not take advantage of them and who might even reciprocate. Interestingly, this *Early Spelke, Later Dweck* developmental pattern may be seen as a kind of ontogenetic reflection of the famous tit-for-tat strategy for cooperation, especially effective in maintaining cooperation in groups over time: you should start out altruistic and then treat others selectively, as they treat you.

But also important are social norms, as modeled for and communicated to young children. As children transform themselves into public persons with their own identities in early childhood, they become concerned with their public reputations, and they are eager to follow and even enforce social norms, including upon themselves in the forms of guilt and shame. Children do not only respect social norms, as is typically argued, due to the benefits of reciprocity and threat of punishment. Instead, they are sensitive from a young age to their own interdependence with others in collaborative activities—a kind of social rationality endemic to shared intentionality—and they value conformity to the group as a marker of group identity. These different forms of "we-ness" are important sources of both their own respect for social norms and their enforcement of social norms on others.

It is interesting in this regard that adults who assume that children are not naturally helpful and cooperative and attempt to make them so through external reinforcements and punishments do not create children who internalize social norms and use them to regulate their own behavior. Much research has shown that so-called inductive parenting—in which adults communicate with children about the effects of their actions on others and about the rationality of cooperative social action—is the most effective parenting style to encourage internalization of societal norms and values. Such inductive parenting works best because it correctly assumes a child is already disposed to make the cooperative choice when the effects of her actions on others and on group functioning are made clear to her. Children are altruistic by nature, and this is a predisposition that (because children are also naturally selfish) adults attempt to nurture.

In the second chapter we turn to the question of how human beings might have become so cooperative evolutionarily—again by comparing humans with their nearest primate relatives. The focus in this case is on mutualistic collaboration as the evolutionary source of human skills and motives for shared intentionality (including conventional communication and social institutions), and I argue that mutualistic collaborative activities were the original source of human altruism as well.

2

From Social Interaction to Social Institutions

The primal scene of morality . . . is not one in which I do something to you or you do something to me, but one in which we do something together.
—Christine Korsgaard

IN THE CONTEMPORARY STUDY OF HUMAN BE-
havioral evolution, the central problem is altruism,
specifically, how it came to be. There is no widely
accepted solution to that question, but there is no
shortage of proposals either. The challenge is that
there must be some way for the sacrificing individual
to not sacrifice herself or her progeny out of existence;
there must be some kind of compensating advantage
for her sacrifice. It has been shown that punishment

of non-cooperators (including negative gossip about reputation) helps to stabilize cooperation—again, in the sense of altruism—but punishment is a public good for which the punished pays the cost and everyone benefits, the so-called second-order problem of altruism. And punishment can do its work only if the punished have a tendency to react by doing "the right thing," so the threat of punishment alone cannot explain the origins of altruism.

I will certainly not solve the evolution-of-altruism problem here. But that is okay because I do not believe it is the central process anyway; that is, I do not believe altruism is the process primarily responsible for human cooperation in the larger sense of humans' tendency and ability to live and operate together in institution-based cultural groups. In this story, altruism is only a bit player. The star is mutualism, in which we all benefit from our cooperation but only if we work together, what we may call collaboration. Free-riding persists here, but in the most concrete cases—where you and I must work together to move a heavy log, for instance—free-riding is not really possible because each of our efforts is required for success, and shirking is immediately apparent. As a side benefit, in the context of a mutualistic effort, my altruism toward you—for example, pointing out a tool that will help you do your job—actually helps me as well, as you doing your job helps us toward our common goal. So mutualism might also be the birthplace of human altruism: a protected environment, as it were, to get people started in that direction.

If we take modern apes in general as the model for humans' last common ancestor with other primates, we have a fairly long path to traverse to get to the kinds of large-scale collaborative activities and cultural institutions that characterize modern human societies. But that is what we will try to do here, albeit sketchily. As a starting point, we know from the work of Joan Silk and others that nonhuman primate societies function in large part on the basis of kinship and nepotism, with a healthy dose of dominance thrown in in most cases. Any cooperation they show will thus most likely be based on kinship or direct reciprocity. And we know from the work of Brian Skyrms that in building human-style collaboration from this ape foundation, we do not face a prisoner's dilemma, in which individuals assess their own benefits versus those of the group. Rather, our scenario is a stag hunt in which everyone prefers to collaborate because of the rewards doing so brings each of us and our compatriots. The problem is how we can get ourselves to join forces. This is not a trivial task since what I do in such situations depends on what I think you will do and vice versa, recursively, which means that we must be able to communicate and trust one another sufficiently. I will call my evolutionary hypothesis the *Silk for Apes, Skyrms for Humans* hypothesis.

To get from ape group activities to human collaboration, we need three basic sets of processes. First and most importantly, early humans had to evolve some serious social-cognitive skills and motivations for coordinating and communicating with others in complex ways involving joint goals and coordinated division of labor among the various roles—what I will call skills and motivations for shared intentionality. Second, to even begin these complex collaborative activities, early humans had first to become more tolerant and trusting of one another than are modern apes, perhaps especially in the context of food. And third, these more tolerant and collaborative humans had to develop some group-level, institutional practices involving public social norms and the assignment of deontic status to institutional roles. But before focusing on these three processes in turn, let us first characterize the starting and ending points of our hypothetical evolutionary pathway a bit more concretely.

A CONCRETE EXAMPLE ANCHORS THE TWO END-points of our evolutionary story: foraging versus shopping. When humans go foraging for nuts in the forest, it is much the same as when chimpanzees do so. Both humans and apes understand the spatial layout of the forest, the causality involved in using tools to extract food, and the goal-directed agency of their companions. But what about when humans go foraging for food in the supermarket? Certain things happen here that do not happen in chimpanzee foraging—they cannot happen in chimpanzee foraging because they are constituted by processes that go beyond purely individual cognition and motivation.

Let us suppose a scenario as follows. We enter the store, pick up a few items, stand in line at the checkout, hand the clerk a credit card to pay, take our items, and leave. This could be described in chimpanzee terms fairly simply as going somewhere, fetching objects, and returning to the place whence one came. But humans understand shopping, more or less explicitly, on a whole other level, on the level of institutional reality. First, entering the store subjects me to a whole set of rights and obligations: I have the right to purchase items for the posted price and the obligation to not steal or destroy items, because they are the property of the store owner. Second, I can expect the items to be safe to eat because the government has a department that ensures this; if a good proves unsafe, I can sue someone. Third, money has a whole institutional structure behind it that everyone trusts so much that they hand over goods for this special paper, or even for electronic marks somewhere coming from my credit card. Fourth, I stand in line in deference to widely held norms, and if I try to jump the line people will rebuke me, I will feel guilty, and my reputation as a nice person will suffer. I could go on listing, practically indefinitely, all of the institutional realities inhabiting the public sphere, realities that foraging chimpanzees presumably do not experience at all.

What is common to all of these institutional phenomena is a uniquely human sense of "we," a sense of shared intentionality. And it does not come only from the collective, institutional world of supermarkets, private property, health departments, and the like. This sense can be seen—perhaps even a bit more sharply—in simpler social interactions. Suppose you and I agree to walk to the store together. Along the way, I suddenly, without warning, veer off and go my own way, leaving you standing there alone. You are not only surprised, but miffed (or maybe worried about me), so that when you return home you will tell your friends about the incident. "We" were walking to the store together, and I broke that "we" unilaterally, due to either my selfishness or my derangement. Interestingly, I could have avoided the whole incident by simply "taking leave," saying that I just remembered something important I had to do, asking permission, as it were, to break our "we."

This sense that we are doing something together—which creates mutual expectations, and even rights and obligations—is, one could argue, uniquely human, even in this simple case. Searle, among others, has shown how the sense of acting together can scale up to the kinds of collective intentionality involved in doing something as institutionally complex as shopping at a supermarket, which exists on the basis of rights, obligations, money, and governments, which in turn exist because "we" all believe and act as if they do.[1] The upshot is that human beings live not only in the physical and social worlds of other apes, but also in an institutional or cultural world of their own making, a world that is populated with all kinds of deontically empowered entities. The specifics of this world vary greatly among different groups of people, but all groups of people live in some such world.

Although many observable features of the human cultural world clearly differentiate it from the primate social world, identifying the psychological processes underlying these features is far from straightforward. The approach in our laboratory has been to identify differences in the ways that great apes and young children engage with others socially as they collaborate and communicate with them in relatively simple situations. I will concentrate on the three sets of processes noted above, in turn:

(1) coordination and communication

(2) tolerance and trust

(3) norms and institutions

And, to keep things relatively simple and focused,

I will tell my evolutionary tales mostly in the context of foraging for food, as I have come to believe that many of the key steps in the evolution of human cooperation had to do with how individuals deal with each other in the context of procuring their daily bread.[2]

Coordination and Communication

All social animals are, by definition, cooperative in the sense of living together relatively peacefully in groups. Most social species forage as a group in one way or another, mainly as a defense against predation. In many mammalian species, individuals also form specific relationships with other individuals, leading to coalitions and alliances in their intra-group competition for food and mates. Inter-group defense and defense against predators is also a group activity among many mammalian species. Chimpanzees and other great apes do more or less all of these group things, so our question is how their collective activities are similar to and different from human forms of collaboration.

In "shared cooperative activities,"[3] the collaborators must first of all be mutually responsive to one another's intentional states. But beyond this minimal requirement, the two key characteristics are: (1) the participants have a joint goal in the sense that we (in mutual knowledge) do X together; and (2) the participants coordinate their roles—their plans and sub-plans of action, including helping the other in her role as needed—which are interdependent. Establishing a joint goal constitutes a kind of coordination problem by itself and therefore requires some specific forms of communication.[4]

The most complex collaborative activity in which chimpanzees engage in the wild is their group hunting of red colobus monkeys in the trees of the Tai Forest in Côte d'Ivoire. The chimpanzees have a shared goal and take complementary roles in their hunting. One individual, called the driver, chases the prey in a certain direction, while others, so-called blockers, climb the trees and prevent the prey from changing direction. An ambusher then moves in front of the prey, foreclosing escape.[5] Of course, when the hunting event is described with this vocabulary of complementary roles, it appears to be a truly collaborative activity: complementary roles imply that there is a joint goal. The question, however, is whether this vocabulary is appropriate.

I believe there is a more plausible characterization of this hunting activity. The hunt commences when one male chimpanzee begins chasing a monkey through the trees, with the understanding that fellow chimpanzees, who are necessary for success, are in the area. Each other chimpanzee then takes, in turn, the most opportune spatial position still available at any given moment in the emerging hunt. The second chimpanzee blocks the fleeing monkey, the third goes to a plausible other escape route, others stay on the ground in case the monkey drops down. In this process, each participant is attempting to maximize its own chances of catching the prey, without any prior joint goal or plan or assignment of roles. This kind of hunting event clearly is a group activity of some complexity, in which individuals are mutually responsive to one another's spatial position as they encircle the prey. But wolves and lions do something very similar, and most researchers do not attribute to them any kind of joint goals or plans. The apes are engaged in a group activity in I-mode, not in We-mode.[6]

As opposed to the chimpanzees' group activity in I-mode, human children, from soon after their first birthdays, work in We-mode, forming a joint goal with their partner. This is clearest in a comparative study in which Warneken and fellow researchers presented 14-to-24-month-old children and three human-raised, juvenile chimpanzees with four collaborative activities: two instrumental tasks in which there was a concrete goal and two social games in which there was no concrete goal other than playing the collaborative game itself. The human-adult partner was instructed to cease participating in the tasks at some point as a way of determining subjects' understanding of the adult's commitment to the joint activity.

Results were clear and consistent. The chimpanzees showed no interest in the social games, basically declining to participate. In the problem-solving tasks, on the other hand, they synchronized their behavior relatively skillfully with that of the human, as shown by the fact that they were often successful in bringing about the desired result. However, when the human partner stopped participating, no chimpanzee ever made a communicative attempt to reengage her—even in cases where they were seemingly highly motivated to obtain the goal—suggesting that they had not formed with her a joint goal. In contrast, the human children collaborated in the social games as well as the instrumental tasks. Indeed, they sometimes turned the instrumental tasks into social games by placing the obtained reward back into the apparatus to start the activity again; the collaborative activity itself was more rewarding than the instrumental goal. Most importantly, when the adult stopped participating in the activity, the children actively encouraged him to reengage by communicating with him in some way, suggesting that they had formed with him a shared goal to which they now wanted him to recommit.[7]

Two other experiments from our lab further demonstrate children's ability to commit to a joint goal. The first tested the idea that neither partner in a collaborative activity is satisfied until both have gotten their reward: the joint goal is not achieved unless both partners benefit. Researchers had a pair of three-year-old children work fairly hard to lift and move a pole up a step-like apparatus, one child on each end of the pole. Attached to each end was a bowl with a reward credit that could be cashed in a few feet away. The trick was that one child's reward became available to her first, through a hole in the Plexiglas covering the steps. Children in this position took their reward, but then noticed that for the other child to get her reward, they needed to work together for one more step. Some of the fortunate children cashed in their reward credit first, but then they returned to collaborate on the final step to make sure that the less fortunate child got hers. Other fortunate children even waited and helped the unrewarded child before cashing in their own reward. Overall, most of the children seemed to feel committed to their joint goal—completing the task so that both got their reward—much more than in a control condition involving simply helping the other in this same context but with no collaboration.[8]

In the second experiment, researchers had an adult and a child begin a collaborative activity with an explicit joint commitment. The adult said something like "Hey. Let's go play that game. Okay?" Only when the child explicitly agreed did they proceed to play the game together. In a control condition, the child began playing the game on her own, and the adult joined her unbidden. In both conditions the adult then stopped playing for no reason. Three-year-old children (but not two-year-old children) behaved differently depending on whether they and the adult had made an explicit commitment. If the adult had made an explicit commitment, then the child was more demanding that the adult return to the activity—after all, the two had agreed to play the game together. Moreover, in a variation on this procedure, when researchers enticed the child away from the shared activity (with an even more fun game across the room), those who had made an explicit commitment with the adult were much more likely than the others to take leave from her by, for example, saying something to her, handing her the toy, or looking to her face before departing.[9] They knew that they were breaking a commitment and attempted to ease the blow by acknowledging it first.

In addition to a joint goal, a fully collaborative activity requires that there be some division of labor and that each partner understand the other's role. In another study, a research team engaged in a collaborative activity with very young children, around eighteen months of age, and then exchanged roles with the children on the next turn, forcing the children into a role they had never played. Even these very young children readily adapted to the new role, suggesting that in their initial joint activity with the adult, they had understood the adult's perspective and role.[10] Three young, human-raised chimpanzees did not reverse roles in the same way.[11] Our interpretation is that this role reversal signals that the human infants understood the joint activity from a "bird's-eye view," with the joint goal and complementary roles all in a single representational format (similar to Nagel's "view from nowhere"). In contrast, the chimpanzees understood their own action from a first-person perspective and that of the partner from a third-person perspective, but they did not have a bird's-eye view of the activity and roles. Thus, from the perspective of both participants, human collaborative activities are performed through generalized roles potentially filled by anyone, including the self. Some philosophers call these "agent-neutral roles."

As individuals coordinate their actions with one another in collaborative activities, they also coordinate their attention. Indeed, in the child-development literature, the earliest collaborative activities are often called "joint attentional activities." At about nine months of age, infants begin to do things with adults like roll a ball back and forth or stack blocks together—activities that involve a very simple joint goal. As the children play, they monitor the adult and her attention, and the adult monitors the child and the child's attention. No one is certain how best to characterize this potentially infinite recursion of monitoring, but it seems to be part of infants' experience—in some nascent form—from before the first birthday. However it is best characterized, the attentional loop initially is made possible by having a joint goal. If we both know that we have the joint goal of making this tool together, then it is relatively easy for each of us to know where the other's attention is focused because the locus of attention is the same for both of us: we are focused on that which is relevant to our goal. Later in life, infants can enter into joint attention without a joint goal. For example, if a loud noise is heard, the infant and the adult can attend to it together, what we have called bottom-up joint attention, since it begins with an attention-grabbing event. But in the beginning, in both phylogeny and ontogeny, joint attention only happens in the context of a joint goal, what we have called top-down joint attention, since actors' goals determine attention.

In collaborative activities, participants not only jointly pay attention to matters relevant to the common goal, but they each have their own perspective as well. Indeed, the whole notion of perspective depends on first having a joint attentional focus that we may then view differently (otherwise we just see completely different things). This dual-level attentional structure—shared focus of attention at a higher level, differentiated into perspectives at a lower level—is directly parallel to the dual-level intentional structure of the collaborative activity itself (shared goal with individual roles) and ultimately derives from it.[12]

Perspective in joint attention plays a critical role in human communication. To illustrate, consider an experiment with one-year-old children. An adult entered the room, looked at the side of a complex toy from a moderate distance, and said "Oh! Cool! Look at that!" For some of the children, this was their first encounter with the adult, so they assumed she was reacting to this cool toy she was seeing for the first time. But other children had previously joined the adult in playing with this complex toy extensively. The toy was thus old news, a part of their common ground. In this case the children assumed that the adult could not be talking about the whole object—one does not emote excitedly to another about something that is well-known to both. The children assumed that the adult was excited about either some other object or some other aspect of the toy.[13]

By all indications—including several experiments that looked quite carefully for it[14]—great apes do not engage in joint attention. Various data show that a chimpanzee knows that his group-mate sees the monkey,[15] but there is no evidence that the chimpanzee knows that his group-mate sees him seeing the monkey. That is, there is no evidence that great apes can do even one step of recursive mind reading (if you will allow me this term), which is the cognitive underpinning of all forms of common conceptual ground. If, as we hypothesize, the first step on the way to what has been called mutual knowledge, common knowledge, joint attention, mutual cognitive environment, intersubjectivity, and so forth, was taken in collaborative activities with joint goals, the reason that great apes do not establish joint attention with others is that they do not participate in activities with joint goals in the first place.[16] In our several collaboration studies with great apes, they have never made any attempt at overt communication to establish joint goals and attention, whereas human children engage in all kinds of verbal and nonverbal communication for forming joint goals and attention and for coordinating their various roles in the activity.

Human cooperative communication thus evolved first within the bounds of collaborative activities because these activities provided the needed common ground for establishing joint topics, and because they generated the cooperative motives that Grice[17] established as essential if the inferential machinery is to work appropriately. Consider, once again, the most basic of uniquely human communicative acts: the pointing gesture. Outside of any shared context, pointing means nothing. But if we are in the midst of a collaborative activity (say, gathering nuts), the pointing gesture is most often immediately and unambiguously meaningful ("there's a nut"). As Wittgenstein first noted, I may point to a piece of paper, its color, its shape, or any of its many different aspects, depending on the *lebensform* (form of life) in which the communicative act is embedded.[18] Making contact with some lebensform—a collaborative activity would be a prototype, perhaps—grounds the act of pointing in a shared social practice, which gives meaning to the otherwise empty gesture. And without this grounding, conventional communication using "arbitrary" linguistic symbols is simply noise. Only some time after humans had developed means of cooperative communication within collaborative activities did they begin to communicate cooperatively outside of such activities.

To sum up, the species-unique structure of human collaborative activities is that of a joint goal with individual roles, coordinated by joint attention and individual perspectives. It was by way of Skyrms's stag hunt[19] that human beings evolved skills and motivations for engaging in these kinds of activities for concrete mutualistic gains. Skills and motivations for cooperative communication coevolved with these collaborative activities because such communication both depended on these activities and contributed to them by facilitating the coordination needed to co-construct a joint goal and differentiated roles. My hypothesis is that concrete collaborative activities of the type we see today in young children are mostly representative of the earliest collaborative activities in human evolution. They have the same basic structure as the collaborative hunting of large game or the collaborative gathering of fruit in which one individual helps the other climb the tree and procure the food they will later share. Indeed, I believe that the ecological context within which these skills and motivations developed was a sort of cooperative foraging. Humans were put under some kind of selective pressure to collaborate in their gathering of food—they became obligate collaborators—in a way that their closest primate relatives were not.[20]

For those who need something a bit more concrete than the observation and analysis of behavior and cognition, consider that humans have a physiological characteristic that is highly unusual and potentially connected to their cooperativeness. All 200-plus species of nonhuman primates have basically dark eyes, with the sclera—commonly called the "white of the eye"—barely visible. The sclera of humans (i.e., the visible part) is about three times larger, making the direction of human gaze much more easily detectable by others. A recent experiment showed that in following the gaze direction of others, chimpanzees rely almost exclusively on head direction—they follow an experimenter's head direction up even if the experimenter's eyes are closed—whereas human infants rely mainly on eye direction—they follow an experimenter's eyes, even if the head stays stationary.[21] Evolutionarily, you can readily imagine why it is beneficial for you to be able to follow my eye direction easily—to spy distant predators and food, for example—but nature cannot select the whiteness of my eyes based on some advantage to you; it must be of some advantage (or at least no disadvantage) to me. In what we call the cooperative-eye hypothesis, my team has argued that advertising my eye direction for all to see could only have evolved in a cooperative social environment in which others were not likely to exploit it to my detriment. Thus, one possibility is that eyes that facilitated others' tracking of one's gaze evolved in cooperative social groups in which monitoring one another's attentional focus was to everyone's benefit in completing joint tasks.

Tolerance and Trust

I am focusing here on collaborative activities as the key to many qualities uniquely human. But in an evolutionary story, collaborative activities actually constitute a kind of middle step; there is an earlier development that paved the way for the evolution of complex collaborative activities. None of the advancements in cooperation we have been talking about could get moving evolutionarily in animals that were always competing: there had to be some initial emergence of tolerance and trust—in our current story, around food—to put a population of our ancestors in a position where selection for sophisticated collaborative skills was viable.

In the standard evolutionary explanation of sociality, animal species become social in order to protect against predation. Typically, defense is best achieved in groups. When protection is not needed, individuals are better off foraging for food on their own because then they do not have to compete with others for food constantly. When food is dispersed, there are generally no problems: antelope graze peacefully across the fertile plains, staying together for protection. But when food is found in clumps, dominance raises its ugly head. When a primate group finds a tree full of fruit, there is typically both scramble and competition, and individuals separate themselves from others by at least a few meters as they eat. The paradigmatic clumped source of food is the prey animal. For solitary hunters, of course, prey animals present no competition-related problems. But for social carnivores such as lions and wolves, a group kill raises the issue of how to share the spoils. The solution is that the carcass is large enough that even while some individuals may get more, each individual still gets plenty. In the case where one individual actually makes the final kill, as the others approach the carcass the killer must allow them to have some because attempting to fend off one competitor would mean losing the carcass to others (this is the so-called tolerated-theft model of food sharing).

Chimpanzees make their living mainly off of fruits and other vegetation. Fruits tend to be a loosely clumped, highly valued resource, so they spur competition. But some chimpanzees also engage in the aforementioned group hunting for red colobus monkeys. As noted, this group hunting appears truly collaborative, with shared goals and a division of labor. When the monkey is captured, the hunters get more of the meat than do bystanders who did not hunt. This supports the idea of a shared goal with a fair division of spoils.[22] But recent research demonstrates otherwise. First of all, the chimpanzee who actually makes the kill immediately attempts to avoid others by stealing away from the kill site, if possible, or by climbing to the end of a branch to restrict the access of other chimpanzees. But in most cases, meat possessors are unsuccessful in attempts to hoard, and are surrounded by beggars, who begin pulling on the meat. The possessor typically allows the beggars to take some meat, and researchers have documented quantitatively that this largesse is a direct response to begging and harassment: the more a beggar begs and harasses, the more food he gets. The stridency of the harassment may be thought of as an index of how strongly the harasser would be willing to fight, and this willingness to fight may derive, at least in part, from the excitement of the hunt. There is also the related possibility that even unsuccessful hunters obtain more meat than latecomers because hunters are the first ones immediately at the carcass and begging, whereas latecomers are relegated to the second ring.[23]

This account of chimpanzee group hunting is supported by the Melis study described in the first chapter. Recall that researchers presented two chimpanzees with out-of-reach food that could only be obtained if each pulled simultaneously on one of the two ropes available (attached to a platform with food on it). The main finding was that when there were two piles of food, one in front of each participant, there was a good amount of synchronized pulling and, therefore, success. However, when there was only one pile of food in the middle of the platform, making it difficult to share at the end, cooperation fell apart almost completely. In general, chimpanzees are so competitive over food that they can only coordinate synchronized activities when the division-of-spoils problem is somehow ameliorated. In a similar experiment with bonobos—our other closest living relative, with a reputation for being more cooperative than chimpanzees—there was a bit more tolerance for sharing clumped piles of food, but not so much more.[24]

In the case of children—who have also been studied using this method—the clumped food did not bother the subjects at all. Indeed they worked out various ways for dividing it up with almost no squabbling. (I guess I should note for everyone with multiple children that these were not pairs of siblings.) Interestingly, in this situation children sometimes challenge one another over issues of fairness. In one trial, one of the children took all of the candies that she and her partner reeled in together. The deprived child then challenged, and the greedy child immediately relented. Researchers saw no challenges when the two children procured equal shares.

In ongoing trials this study has been extended to examine various kinds of collective action problems. For example, subjects pull in a board with two sets of rewards on it, but in some cases the distribution of food is highly asymmetrical—five for me and one for you; six for me and none for you. Without some arrangement for dividing rewards more fairly, collaboration will fall apart over time. And this is exactly the experience of the chimpanzees. After helping for a trial or two without reward, the unlucky chimpanzee refuses to continue helping, and the effort fails. Typically, the one who ends up with the food does not share it, forestalling further cooperation. The hypothesis is that the children will find various ways of dividing rewards more fairly in order to keep the collaboration going across trials.

These studies suggest that humans and chimpanzees compete for food with starkly different levels of intensity. For humans to have evolved complex skills and motivations for collaborative activities in which everyone benefits, there had to have been an initial step that broke us out of the great-ape pattern of strong competition for food, low tolerance for food sharing, and no food offering at all. It is relatively easy for chimpanzees to collaborate in the "large carcass" scenario in which each individual has a reasonable probability of capturing the monkey, and even unsuccessful participants can still harass the capturer and get some meat. But how can there be a joint goal—in the human sense—of capturing a monkey when the hunters know that success will invariably provoke a contest for the booty?

There are a number of evolutionary hypotheses about the context in which humans became more socially tolerant and less competitive over food. We could tell a story totally within the context of foraging, such that as collaboration became obligatory, those individuals who already were less competitive with food and more tolerant of others naturally had an adaptive advantage (assuming they could find one another, as Skyrms has shown).

We could also speculate that since hunter-gatherer societies tend to be egalitarian, with bullies often ostracized or killed, humans underwent a kind of self-domestication process in which very aggressive and acquisitive individuals were weeded out by the group.[25]

Finally, we could argue for the importance of so-called cooperative breeding (cooperative childcare). It is a startling fact that among all of the great-ape species except humans, the mother provides basically 100 percent of childcare. Among humans, across traditional and modern societies, the average figure is closer to 50 percent. In a cooperative-breeding scenario, helpers—all those who are not the mother—often engage in a variety of pro-social behaviors such as active food provisioning and basic childcare. In *Mothers and Others*, Sarah Hrdy argues that this changed social context, which may have arisen due to differences in the way humans needed to forage and the monogamous relationships between females and males, created humans' unique pro-social motivations.[26]

It is of course possible that all of the above scenarios played a role. The important point is simply that there was some initial step in human evolution away from great apes, involving the emotional and motivational side of experience, that propelled humans into a new adaptive space in which complex skills and motivations for collaborative activities and shared intentionality could be selected.

When we are engaged in a mutually beneficial collaborative activity, when I help you play your role either through physical help or by informing you of something useful, I am helping myself, as your success in your role is critical to our overall success. Mutualistic activities thus provide a protected environment for the initial steps in the evolution of altruistic motives. Conditions that enable individuals to extend their helpful attitudes outside of this protected environment must then evolve. To explain this subsequent evolutionary step, we must invoke the usual suspects: reciprocity and reputation leading the way, followed by punishment and social norms. Creating altruistic motives, sui generis, outside of mutualistic activities—and outside of kin-selection contexts, which may have been the protected environment for other primates—would be extremely difficult, if not impossible. But generalizing preexisting motives to new individuals and contexts is not nearly so evolutionarily problematic. If the right conditions arise, the cognitive and motivational machinery is already there.

Norms and Institutions

If we were thinking in terms of an evolutionary story, at this point we would have hominids who were more tolerant and trusting of one another than are modern-day great apes and who had more powerful skills and motivations for shared intentionality and collaboration. But to complete the picture—to get from foraging to shopping—we need some group-level processes; specifically, we need social norms and institutions.

As I argued in the first chapter, I do not believe that great apes have any social norms, if we mean by this socially agreed-upon and mutually known expectations bearing social force, monitored and enforced by third parties. But in recent studies my colleagues and I have documented two related behaviors in our primate ancestors. In another version of the mutualistic, pulling-a-plank task, our team gave chimpanzees a choice of collaborative partners, one of whom the researchers knew from previous testing to be a very good collaborator and one of whom they knew was very poor. The subject apes quickly learned which was which, and they avoided choosing the poor collaborator.[27] Of course, the subjects were simply trying to maximize their own gains from the collaboration and had no thought of punishing the poor collaborator. But such choices—in what some have called a "biological market"—serve to discourage poor collaborators nonetheless, as they are excluded from beneficial opportunities. Such exclusion may thus be seen as a forerunner to punishment.

In a different study in our lab, researchers have shown that if one chimpanzee steals food from another, the victim will retaliate by preventing the thief from keeping and eating the food. But so far in ongoing research we have not witnessed any comparable behavior from observers. Individuals do not try to prevent a thief from enjoying his bounty (or to inflict any other kind of negative sanction) if he stole it from someone else. Despite ongoing efforts, we have observed no third-party punishment. While these two great-ape behaviors—excluding and retaliating—serve to discourage antisocial behavior among group-mates, in neither case is any kind of social norm being applied, certainly not in any agent-neutral sense from a third-party stance.[28]

In contrast, humans operate with two basic types of social norms, though many norms are hybrids: norms of cooperation (including moral norms) and norms of conformity (including constitutive rules).

Norms of cooperation presumably emanate historically from situations in which individuals going about their daily business, in either individualistic or mutualistic situations, bump into one another in some way. Through processes that we do not understand very well, mutual expectations arise, and perhaps individuals try to induce others to behave differently,[29] or they agree in an egalitarian manner to behave in certain ways, such that some kind of equilibrium results. To the extent that this equilibrium is governed by mutually recognized expectations of behavior that all individuals cooperate in enforcing, we may begin to speak of social norms or rules.

I will not pretend that I have any fundamentally new answers to this, one of the most fundamental questions in all of the social sciences: where do these cooperative norms come from and how do they work? I only propose that the kinds of collaborative activities in which young children today engage are the natural cradle of social norms of the cooperative variety. This is because they contain the seeds of the two key ingredients. First, social norms have force. This can come from the threat of punishment for norm violators, but norms have a rational dimension as well. In mutualistic collaborative activities, we both know together that we both depend on one another for reaching our joint goal. This basically transforms the individual normativity of rational action—to achieve this goal, I should do X (characteristic of all cognitively guided organisms)—into a kind of social normativity of joint rational action—to achieve our joint goal, I should do X, and you should do Y. If you don't do Y, the cause of our failure is your behavior, and that makes me angry at you. If I don't do my part, again we fail, but in this case I feel sympathy for your plight (and maybe anger at myself). The force of cooperative norms thus comes from our mutually recognized interdependence and our natural reactions to the failures of both ourselves and others.

Social disapproval is still not a cooperative social norm, because it lacks the second key ingredient: generality. Normative judgments, by definition, require some generalized standard to which an individual's specific activities are compared. Some collaborative activities in a community are performed over and over by various members of a social group, with different individuals in different roles on different occasions, such that the collaborative activities become cultural practices whose structures —in terms of the joint goals and the various roles involved—everyone knows mutually. To gather honey from beehives in trees, for instance, one person stands next to the tree, another climbs on her shoulders and gathers the honey from the hive and hands it down, and a third pours the honey into a vessel. As novices tag along and socially learn what to do in the different roles in this activity, the roles become defined in a general way, such that there are mutual expectations in the group that anyone playing role X must do certain things in order to achieve group success. Any praise or blame for an individual in a particular role is offered in the context of the standard that everyone mutually knows must be met. Thus, social practices in which "we" act together interdependently in interchangeable roles toward a joint goal generate, over time, mutual expectations leading to generalized, agent-neutral normative judgments.

To illustrate broadly the birth of a social practice and its normative dimension, I shall briefly describe a typical scene from one of our helping experiments. To begin, the child watches passively as the adult puts magazines away in the cabinet. Then, on the second round, when the adult has trouble with the doors because his hands are full of magazines, the child helps him open the doors. Then, having figured out the process, in the third round the child anticipates everything, opening the door in advance and leading the way in the collaborative activity of putting away the magazines. In some cases the child even directs the adult in where to put the magazines (by pointing). Over the three enactments of this activity, the child and adult develop mutual expectations about one another's behavior, such that the child ends up structuring the activity and even communicating to the adult something like "They go there," meaning that, in this activity, certain tasks are performed according to normative requirements. It is noteworthy for our evolutionary story that this child is only eighteen months of age, barely verbal, and not really using any normative language at all (and indeed the normative interpretation I have given his pointing is not the only possible one). But still, from all of our studies, it seems clear that on the basis of just one or a few experiences in a collaborative activity with an adult, children readily conclude that this is how it is done, this is how "we" do it.

In addition to norms of cooperation, human behavior is guided through norms of conformity or conventionality. At some point in human evolution, it became important for individuals in a group to all behave alike; there arose pressure to conform. The proximate motivation here is to be like others, to be accepted in the group, to be one of the "we" that constitutes the group and that competes with other groups. If we are to function as a group, we must do things in ways that have proven effective in the past, and we must distinguish ourselves from others who do not know our ways. It may be that imitation and conformity were in many ways the central processes that led humans in new directions evolutionarily.[30] The reason is that imitation and conformity can create high degrees of intra-group homogeneity and inter-group heterogeneity, and on a faster time scale than that of biological evolution. Because of this peculiar fact—presumably characteristic of no other species—a new process of cultural group selection became possible. Human social groups became maximally distinctive from one another in language, dress, and customs, and they competed with one another. Those with the most effective social practices thrived relative to others. This is presumably the source of humans' in-group, out-group mentality, which researchers have shown is operative even in very young infants (who, for example, prefer to interact with people who speak their own language even before they themselves speak).[31]

Both norms of cooperation and conformity are cemented by guilt and shame, which presuppose some kind of social norms, or at least social judgments, and so co-evolutionary processes between biology and culture.[32] UCLA anthropologist Robert Boyd has argued with great insight that punishment and norms turn problems of competition (as in mixed-motive games, such as the prisoner's dilemma) into problems of coordination. Without punishment and norms, an individual actor is thinking mostly of how he can get some food (and perhaps even how others can get some food as well). But with punishment and norms, he must also think about how potential punishers and gossips expect and desire him to share any food he might procure, so he must, in effect, coordinate with their expectations and desires if he wants to avoid punishment. Internalized social norms, with accompanying guilt and shame, ensure that coordination with the group's expectations need not involve any overt behavior.

MICHAEL TOMASELLO   95

Norms provide the background of trust in which agent-neutral roles and shared cooperative activities with joint goals and joint attention enable social institutions. But the kind of conventionally created realities characteristic of social institutions depend on one more ingredient: a special kind of imagination and symbolic communication. The origin of symbolic communication is a long story.[33] It depended most fundamentally on cooperative ways of performing tasks and began with the pointing gesture inside joint attentional activities. But there arose a need to communicate about things not in the here and now, which gave birth to iconic gestures (not yet conventionalized) in which I pantomime some scene for you in a kind of pretense display. Iconic gestures are "naturally" interpretable by humans (i.e., those who already understand the Gricean communicative intention, which arose in association with the pointing gesture), who readily see the actions of others as intentionally directed toward outcomes.

Among children, what we first see of this is pretend play. And contrary to its reputation as a solitary activity—which it may be in older children—the origins of play (at least the acting out of scenes for others) are inherently social. Children form with another person a joint commitment to treat this stick as a horse. Here they have created a status function. Such status functions, socially created in pretense, are precursors ontogenetically and perhaps phylogenetically to collective agreement that this piece of paper is money, or that that person is president, with all of the rights and obligations those agreements entail.[34] An important recent study has demonstrated that these jointly assigned status functions carry normative force even among young children. In this study children agreed with the adult that one object was bread to eat and another was soap for cleaning up the relationship between the actual objects and their putative purposes was imagined in both cases. When a puppet confused the agreed-upon assignments by trying to eat the soap, the children objected strenuously.[35] We have agreed that this object will be the bread and this will be the soap, and any violation of this must be corrected.

Joint agreement among children that a wooden block is a bar of soap thus constitutes a step on the way to the human institutional reality in which objects and behaviors are given special deontic status by some form of collective agreement and practice. These joint agreements are different from the typical social norms governing overt social behavior in that they begin with a conventionally created symbolic reality—the pretend or institutional scenario—and then collectively assign deontic powers to the relevant roles and entities within that symbolic scenario.

MY SILK FOR APES, SKYRMS FOR HUMANS hypothesis is that in order to have created the ways of life that they have, *Homo sapiens* must have begun with collaborative activities of a kind that other primates simply are not equipped for either emotionally or cognitively. Specifically, humans came to engage in collaborative activities with a joint goal and distinct and generalized roles, with participants mutually aware that they were dependent on one another for success. These activities hold the seeds of generalized, agent-neutral normative judgments of rights and responsibilities, as well as various kinds of division of labor and status assignments as seen in social institutions. They also are the birthplace of human altruistic acts, and humans' uniquely cooperative forms of communication. Humans putting their heads together in shared cooperative activities are thus the originators of human culture. How and why all of this arose in human evolution is unknown, but one speculation is that in the context of foraging for food (both hunting and gathering), humans were forced to become cooperators in a way that other primates were not.

Of course, humans are not cooperating angels; they also put their heads together to do all kinds of heinous deeds. But such deeds are not usually done to those inside "the group." Indeed, recent evolutionary models have demonstrated what politicians have long known: the best way to motivate people to collaborate and to think like a group is to identify an enemy and charge that "they" threaten "us." The remarkable human capacity for cooperation therefore seems to have evolved mainly for interactions within the local group. Such group-mindedness in cooperation is, perhaps ironically, a major cause of strife and suffering in the world today. The solution—more easily described than attained—is to find new ways to define the group.

3

Where Biology and Culture Meet

IF EVOLUTIONARY SUCCESS IS MEASURED IN terms of population size, then humans became especially successful, relative to other great apes, only very recently. Specifically, the number of humans began to rise dramatically only about ten thousand years ago, with the rise of agriculture and cities. These provoked all kinds of new cooperative organizations and problems, leading to everything from cost accounting of the food stores, legal systems to protect private property, social class as a way of organizing division of labor, religious rituals to promote group cohesion, and on and on until we reach contemporary industrial society with all of its mind-boggling complexities.

However, the changes we see in human societies beginning with the advent of agriculture and cities are not due, on anyone's account, to any kind of biological adaptation. The changes would seem to be sociological only, given their recency and the fact that by this time modern humans were already spread out all over the globe (so that a species-wide biological change was highly unlikely).[1] What this means is that most, if not all, of the highly complex forms of cooperation in modern industrial societies—from the United Nations to credit card purchases over the Internet—are built primarily on cooperative skills and motivations biologically evolved for small-group interactions: the kinds of altruistic and collaborative activities that we have seen here in our simple studies of great apes and young children.

But already in these kinds of small-group interactions we see fundamental differences between human children and apes. From very early in ontogeny, human children are altruistic in ways that chimpanzees and other great apes are not. Although there is evidence that chimpanzees sometimes help others attain their goals behaviorally, they are not particularly generous with food (as compared with children and adult humans), and they do not offer information freely to one another though communication that in any way resembles the human variety. In terms of collaboration, again, from very early in ontogeny, human children collaborate with others in ways unique to their species. They form with others joint goals to which both parties are normatively committed, they establish with others domains of joint attention and common conceptual ground, and they create with others symbolic, institutional realities that assign deontic powers to otherwise inert entities. Children are motivated to engage in these kinds of collaborative activities for their own sake, not just for their contribution to individual goals.

Laid on top of all of this, as it were, are social norms. Evolutionarily, humans create—and, ontogenetically, children internalize—mutually expected standards of behavior. Everyone is ready to enforce these standards even through costly (altruistic) punishment. First came norms of cooperation, built on interdependence with collaborative partners, and also on reciprocity and respect for others as beings like oneself. Then came norms of conformity, built on a need to belong to the social group and to identify with it—or else risk ostracism—and to distinguish our group from others. Children today respect and internalize both kinds of norms (including many norms with both cooperative and conformist elements) due to external social pressures and to the social rationality of cooperative interactions governed by shared intentionality.

Normal human ontogeny thus involves, necessarily, a cultural dimension that the ontogeny of other primates does not. Individual human beings must learn how others in their culture do things, and moreover, how those others *expect* them to do things. A chimpanzee can develop its species-typical cognitive and social skills in a wide variety of social contexts. But without the human cultural niche, and the skills and motivations for participating in it, a developing human child would not become a normally functioning person at all. Human beings are biologically adapted to grow and develop to maturity within a cultural context. Through our collaborative efforts, we have built our cultural worlds, and we are constantly adapting to them.

II

Forum

Joan B. Silk

IN A TIME WHEN WE HAVE ALL TOO MUCH EVI-
dence of the harm that humans can do to one another
and to the planet, it is ironic that striking developments within the human sciences have highlighted
our capacity for cooperation, our concern for the
welfare of others, and our altruistic social preferences.
It is extremely exciting to see the human sciences
converging on the question of how humans evolved
to be such an altruistic species.

Efforts to answer this question have been illumi-
nated by theoretical, methodological, and empirical
contributions from evolutionary theory, primate be-

havioral ecology, cognitive psychology, developmental psychology, economics, and anthropology. This cross-fertilization means that a primate behavioral ecologist, like me, can borrow methods from behavioral economics to conduct systematic experiments on how children develop altruistic social preferences. It also means that a developmental psychologist, like Michael Tomasello, starts to think about game theory, and an economist, like Ernst Fehr, about the ultimate factors that shape utility functions and how an understanding of human psychology may be as important as an understanding of mathematics in the development of economic theory.

The work being done on children and apes under Tomasello's supervision is a testament to the value of this cross-fertilization among disciplines.

In Chapter 2 Tomasello draws attention to a number of differences between apes and humans that might affect their respective ability to cooperate: apes lack the capacity for joint attention, trust and tolerance are more limited than in human societies, and apes participate much less often in activities that yield group-level benefits. I would add two other items to this list: first, only humans can orchestrate cooperation in large groups of individuals with imperfectly aligned preferences.[1] Second, humans show more concern for the welfare of others (also known as altruistic social preferences) than apes do.[2]

Tomasello argues that the benefits gained from participating in mutualistic endeavors favored the evolution of the distinctive human capacities that he has identified. In this account, altruism plays a minor role. I am not convinced by this argument, and here I will try to explain why.

THE STAG HUNT IS AN EXTREMELY SPECIAL CASE: two hunters working together can take down a stag, while a lone hunter can only catch a single hare.[3] Here the interests of both parties are *perfectly* aligned. Because each player simply decides whether to hunt/not hunt, neither player gains by (a) misinforming his partner about his intentions to hunt or (b) backing off once the hunt has begun. In this game, collaboration is the best possible solution for each partner.

If many situations in nature conformed to the simple payoff scenario of the stag hunt, then cooperation would be ubiquitous. When the interests of the individual and the interests of the group are perfectly aligned, collaboration yields much bigger payoffs than individuals can gain on their own, and there are no selective pressures that threaten to destabilize the interaction.

But circumstances encountered in nature are often not so clear-cut. Cheating is a potential problem whenever the interests of the two parties are not aligned perfectly, and such misalignments are common. This is what I call the *curse of committee work*. It starts in grade school. You are in fifth grade, and the teacher divides you into groups to do reports on Civil War battles. There is always one person in the group who slacks off—he promises to do something, but does not come through. In this case, the interests of individuals are not all aligned—the group wants to produce a great project, but one of its members would rather watch TV than spend time in the library. Committee work is just the adult version of the group project.

We know that cooperation in nonhuman primates is sensitive to potential conflicts of interest. Working with a group of chimpanzees, Meredith Crawford conducted one of the earliest studies of cooperation in nonhuman primates in 1937. Food was placed on top of a box, and two ropes were attached to the box. The box was too far away for the chimps to reach the food, and too heavy for one chimp to pull it forward unassisted. Thus, they had to work together to get the food. Some, but not all, of the pairs that Crawford tested were successful in this task. Using a gauge attached to each rope, Crawford measured the effort that each chimp applied to solving the problem. This is a particularly revealing step in the experiment. Typically, one individual worked much harder than the other. Similarly, as Tomasello points out, when competition for rewards was introduced in the collaboration experiment that Melis and her colleagues conducted, the chimps' ability to solve the task declined markedly.[4] It declined because there was a conflict between the interests of the individual and the joint interests of the pair.

There are actually very few examples of conspecific mutualism. Most of the well-known examples of mutualism involve two different species: lycaenid butterflies and ants, ants and aphids, mycorrhizal fungi and plants, honey bears and honey badgers, cleaner fish and their clients.[5] Even the most complex mutualistic relationships in nature reflect a tug-of-war between collaboration and exploitation.[6] In response, in many mutualistic systems, one or both players have evolved safeguards that ensure that their partners will not cheat. The few cases of mutualism within species involve cooperatively breeding species, such as wild dogs and marmosets, and some cooperative hunters. In most of these cases, groups are composed of closely related individuals, and individual interests are more nearly aligned with the interests of the group. Most forms of cooperation that we see in nature, such as social grooming and alliance formation, are not examples of mutualism: they are examples of altruistic cooperation in which the costs are recouped through reciprocity or nepotism.

The stag hunt is a Rousseauian ideal; perhaps not a common state in nature.

IN COLLABORATIVE RELATIONSHIPS, THE ADAPTIVE challenge is to contend with the incomplete alignment of participants' interests. Even in the best-case scenario for mutualism, the stag hunt, individuals are motivated by the benefits that they will obtain themselves, not by their concern for the welfare of others. Both players decide to participate in the stag hunt because this is the best strategy for each of them, and they do not need to give any consideration to the benefits that their partners will derive in order to decide whether to participate. They need to know what their partners intend to do, but they do not need to place a positive value on the benefits that their partners will receive. So this is a coordination game, where the best strategy for me depends on the strategy of my partner (and vice versa).

A number of experiments from Tomasello's lab have shown that chimpanzees are able to collaborate effectively on joint tasks, but the same chimps show little concern for the welfare of others.[7] Thus, mutualism does not necessarily make you nice. This is because the mindset that you need for mutualistic endeavors may be quite different from the mindset you need for altruistic cooperation. Mutualism is only stable when it represents the best option for the individual, and the interests of the individual are reasonably well aligned with the interests of the group.

Honest communication, mutual trust, and tolerance may be extremely useful for orchestrating mutualistic interactions; but honesty, trust and tolerance are likely to erode if our interests are not perfectly aligned. (I will say that I am going to spend the weekend in the library researching the battle of Gettysburg or working on our committee report, but I am actually going to spend the weekend watching TV or working on my own research.)

Mutualism will not generate concern for the welfare of others. Instead, it will generate manipulative tactics.[8] We don't get from mutualism to Nelson Mandela, we get from mutualism to Niccolò Machiavelli.

Repeat interactions provide one way to generate trust and tolerance. The theory of contingent reciprocity is based on the insight that cooperation between reciprocating partners can be profitable for both individuals—and can be a stable strategy as long as both partners continue to cooperate.[9]

For the female baboons that I study, grooming is mainly directed toward reciprocating partners, often close kin.[10] Grooming is frequently imbalanced within single interactions, as one female may groom her partner considerably more than she is groomed in return on that day.[11] However, over the course of many interactions, these imbalances generally even out. Female baboons form the strongest ties to females with whom they have the most equitable grooming relationships.[12] The most equitable relationships also last longest. Female baboons seem to have solved the trust and tolerance problem through repeat business.

One shortcoming of this mechanism is that it only works in very small groups.[13] Female baboons can form effective partnerships with other females, but they do not form committees.

OF COURSE, NOW WE ARE LEFT WITH THE PUZ-zle of why we are able to cooperate and collaborate. Why do committees function as well as they do? The answer, I think, is that we have altruistic social preferences that motivate us to *value* the benefits to the group.[14] This allows us to align our interests with the interests of the group and to contribute to activities that have group-beneficial outcomes.

This does not mean that we become entirely indifferent to our own preferences and welfare, but it does mean that we place positive weight on outcomes that benefit others. And this leads us to make sacrifices on behalf of others. So we go to committee meetings, we give money to charity, we give blood, we vote, and sometimes we go to war. We also have sanctions that enable us to enforce group-beneficial behavior: laws, fines, gossip, moral sentiments, and the prospect of punishment all support the maintenance of behavior that has group-beneficial outcomes.

These altruistic social preferences are a precondition for the kinds of effective collaboration that humans are so good at. It makes it look as if our joint endeavors are mutualistic stag hunts, when in fact we are often in situations in which our own interests and the interests of the group are imperfectly aligned. I don't give to public radio because my $50 contribution is necessary in order for me to listen to it. I give to public radio because I feel that it is the right thing to do—because it contributes to a public good.

Abraham Lincoln said, "I feel good when I do good," and recent work in neurobiology has confirmed that we find philanthropic acts intrinsically rewarding.[15]

It is the absence of these kinds of social preferences in most other animals that makes it so difficult for mutualism to evolve conspecifically. This may be why chimpanzees are able to cooperate effectively in many contexts, but have not managed to achieve the advantages that "mutualistic" cooperation could provide in their everyday lives (babysitting co-ops, division of labor, more effective hunting tactics, etc). In Tomasello's view, altruistic social preferences arise from the benefits of mutualistic cooperation, but it may be the other way around. There are a number of different explanations of why humans came to have altruistic social preferences: cooperative breeding, cultural group selection, indirect reciprocity, and so on. Once these altruistic social preferences had evolved, they set the stage for the derived features of human cognition and sociality that Tomasello and his colleagues have so carefully documented: shared attention, trust and tolerance, and participation in activities with group-beneficial outcomes.

Carol S. Dweck

MICHAEL TOMASELLO IS A PIONEER, BRAVELY entering territory where others have feared to tread. He not only asks "What makes us uniquely human?" but he also conducts ingenious experiments to support his proposals. And his answer is not just the usual answer—that humans are incredibly smart—but also that we are incredibly nice.

His cutting-edge theory and research has altered the face of developmental psychology by merging cognitive and social development, historically quite separate fields. He has used the child's social nature to illuminate the ways in which the mind develops and culture is transmitted—and, again, he has suggested that what makes us human is not simply a giant brain and its outsized cognitive capacity, but the ability to participate in social interactions of a unique nature. This proposal and the experiments that support it represent an enormous leap forward and have inspired new theories and research that are truly shaking up psychology.

In Chapter 1 Tomasello proposes that from about one year of age young children are *naturally* helpful, informative, and generous and that this is not a product of reward, training, or enculturation. That is, adult influence is not responsible for the helpful disposition of children—it comes naturally. However, later in development, cultural rewards may promote altruism and shape its expression. For example, children's helpfulness may later become governed by such factors as expectation of reciprocity, concern for reputation, and adherence to social norms.

This view he charmingly terms the *Early Spelke, Later Dweck* hypothesis. The hypothesis acknowledges that Elizabeth Spelke has been the grand architect of and foremost contributor to the view that much important early knowledge—termed "core knowledge"—is innate.[1] She has proposed and she and her followers have gathered compelling evidence to show that the child is outfitted with core knowledge about such things as objects, numbers, and space.

I, on the other hand, have mostly studied children's beliefs—things that are constructed or learned; things that are shaped by experience. As may also be implied by the "Later Dweck" part of the hypothesis, I am generally inclined not to rule out learning unless there is a compelling reason to do so. So, true to form, I would like to explore this issue.

The fact that something appears as early as one year of age can be reinterpreted to mean that it appears only after a whole year of experience. And experience can come in many forms aside from direct reward or training. For example, language learning is often ascribed to the working of an innate language module in the brain, and while this may prove true in part, more and more evidence suggests that key aspects of word learning and syntax learning may derive from the statistical patterns inherent in the speech the child hears.[2] In this case, the child learns from input but is not directly rewarded or trained.

Is there evidence that what infants learn during the first year can teach them about altruism and shape altruistic tendencies? It may be that over their first year of life, infants learn to expect that others will or will not be helpful toward them. And different kinds of experiences can indeed shape the young child's own altruism toward others.

I will not argue that expecting help and giving help are not the defaults for infants, but I will suggest that altruism is not a system that has no history of learning and that is impervious to input even in the early days. Now, it is not that I want the whole hypothesis to myself—*Early Dweck, Later Dweck*—but I would like to examine the idea that, although the infant may come prepared for altruism, the flourishing of altruism may be experience-dependent.

My colleague Susan Johnson and her collaborators, in a beautiful program of research, have provided the first evidence that infants learn to expect that their caretaker will or will not come to their aid in times of distress—the first evidence that infants form what John Bowlby, the father of attachment theory, called "working models of relationships." Johnson and her colleagues began by assessing twelve-to-sixteen-month-old infants' relationships with their mothers. That is, using the standard "strange situation" paradigm (in which the infant and mother are separated and reunited to see whether the infant uses the mother as a secure base in times of stress), infants were classified as securely or insecurely attached. Securely attached infants are able to use their mothers as sources of comfort in times of distress, and are generally believed to have had more consistent responsiveness from mothers. In contrast, an insecurely attached infant is not able to derive comfort from the mother's proximity or to recruit the mother to allay distress. Insecurely attached infants are generally believed to have had more unresponsive or inconsistently responsive mothering.

Later, in an infant habituation paradigm, these same infants were shown a film in which figures representing a large "mother" and a small "baby" head up a series of steps. Although the mother climbs easily, the baby is unable to follow her and, stranded at the bottom, lets loose with a heartbreaking cry. Infants were shown this film repeatedly until their interest waned. On the test trials, they were then shown two different endings, one in which the mother returns to the crying baby and another in which she continues up the steps on her own leaving the distressed baby at the bottom.

Which ending "surprised" infants and caused them to look longer? Infant cognition researchers have long used recovery of looking time as evidence that infants see the new stimulus as a violation of their expectations. In this study, the securely attached infants looked longer when the mother kept going, but the insecurely attached infants were more "surprised" when the mother came back. Thus infants with secure and insecure attachment relationships had formed different expectations about whether a caretaker would return and help the child in need.[3]

This research suggests that children may be getting different diets of helpfulness from caretakers—different experiences, different input. Is there any evidence that this will predict different degrees of altruism or helpfulness on the part of these infants toward others? It would be fascinating to see whether generosity, helpfulness, and informativeness appear less frequently in insecurely attached infants, or fall away more readily as the task requires more effort or more sacrifice.

In a dramatic demonstration of the role of experience in infants' altruism, researchers carefully observed the responses of infants and toddlers (one to three years old) in a daycare setting when a nearby peer was in distress.[4] Half of the children in the study were from abusive homes and the other half (matched for age, sex, and race) were from nonabusive homes that were matched as closely as possible for income and stress levels. In response to a peer's distress, the majority of the non-abused infants attended closely to the distressed child, showed concern, or provided comfort.

However, not one of the abused infants showed empathic concern; the most common responses were threats, anger, and even physical assault. It may be that abusive treatment overrides the natural tendency toward altruism, but these data also support the idea that children observe the input from their world telling them how people react to the needs of others.

In the first year of life, parents may indeed be communicating to children what it means to be a good child and a good member of the parent-child dyad, the family, group, or culture. In the case of abused children, parents may be communicating that a good child/person does not cry or otherwise irritate others; that distressed children/people are not deserving of help; and, more generally, that people do not help each other in times of distress. I suggest that from parents' behavior toward the child—altruistic or otherwise—the child may learn how people in the relevant culture behave and are expected to behave toward each other. [5]

Moreover, in my work with toddlers, I have seen that very young children are obsessed with goodness and badness. They are highly concerned with what makes a child good or bad—whether the things they do, the mistakes they make, or the criticisms they receive mean they are good or bad—and what will happen to them if they are good or bad. This may be the *Later Dweck* part of the story, in which children adjust their behavior toward others in light of norms or judgments from others. However, a number of researchers have shown that even infants know that the figure who helps is the "good" one, compared to the figure who hinders another's progress toward a goal. Thus, perhaps quite independently of a systematic and explicit reward regime, children may be highly attuned from a very young age to issues of goodness, and highly motivated to be good children in the way that their culture and experience prescribe. The fact that some forms of good behavior are or become intrinsically motivated for most children would not in itself argue against the role of experience.[6]

At any rate, to argue for a strong form of the Tomasello hypothesis, one would have to establish that there are no processes prior to one year of age in which children are sensitive to the practices, desires, and values of adults and try to act in accordance with them. For these may easily become the child's practices and values—intrinsically rewarding and needing little support from the outside, particularly in simple situations such as the ones tested in Tomasello's interesting studies.

All that said, I am extremely excited by the ideas and the research that Tomasello presents. It is of inestimable importance that someone has had the courage and insight to stake out this domain and to ask those big, big questions. Piaget staked out a new domain and asked new questions. Whether or not he was right in every detail, the field was never the same.

Brian Skyrms

In *Convention* (1969), David Lewis explicitly introduced the notion of common knowledge, which had been tacitly assumed in various ways in classical game theory and which would later become of central importance after the rigorous treatment by the economist Robert J. Aumann. For an item to be common knowledge among a group of agents, it is not enough that everyone know it. Everyone must know it (level 1) and everyone must know that everyone knows it (level 2) and so on for every finite level. For a kind of behavior to be a convention in a community, Lewis requires that it be self-enforcing in a strong way that involves common knowledge.[1] The behavior constituting a convention in force in a community must be such that anyone deviating would be strictly worse off for doing so, and the foregoing must be common knowledge among members of the community. Thus no one has a reason to deviate if others don't, and everyone knows this, and everyone knows all of that, and so forth.

Lewis realized that there appears to be an idealization here—that the common knowledge is 100% common—but he dealt with those who do not have all the requisite knowledge by saying that they are not really members of the relevant community. The convention is maintained by a core community within which there is common knowledge, and hangers-on come along for the ride. He also allowed that individuals may be thought of as having common knowledge if they are capable of reasoning themselves up to an arbitrarily high level of this infinite hierarchy of knowledge.

Grice, in 1967's *Logic and Conversation*, also recognizes the infinite back-and-forth of I-know-that-he-knows-that-I-know…, but on a smaller scale. In conversation, a speaker intends to cause a belief in a listener. But the speaker also wants the listener to know that he is saying what he does with the intention of producing the belief. And the speaker wants the listener to know that he knows that the listener knows. In the pure theory this goes all the way up the ladder, in a way that is aptly captured by Tomasello's phrase "recursive mind reading." Despite some misgivings, there seems to be no natural level at which to stop.

Grice was interested in how information over and above conventional meaning was transferred in conversation. His unifying idea was that conversation is fundamentally a cooperative enterprise, and that the presumption of cooperative intent can be used to extract information. If you tell me you have run out of gas and I say that there is a gas station around the corner, you can presume that the gas station is open or at least that I do not know it to be closed. That is so even though my statement would be literally true in either case. You assume that I am trying to cooperate, and that requires truth but also more than just truth. If I ask you where Peter is, and you answer that he is either in Mexico or Zimbabwe, I can presume that you are not saying this simply because you know that he is in Mexico, although that would make it true. If you are trying to cooperate and know that Peter is in Mexico, you will say so. Grice and followers in this tradition derived various norms of conversation from the presumption of cooperation, which itself was ultimately elaborated in terms of common knowledge of cooperative intentions.[2]

Lewis also bases his account on cooperation. In Lewis's signaling games, the foundation of cooperation is made explicit. It is the strong common interest assumed in the specification of the payoffs. The sender and receiver get the same payoff. If the receiver performs the appropriate act for the state, both sender and receiver are paid. If not, both get nothing. The rules of the game are common knowledge. Thus, it is also common knowledge that it is in the players' interests to cooperate.[3]

Should an account of communication be built on an assumption of common knowledge? There are two reasons to be skeptical. First, it is not credible that groups of animals and of lower organisms have common knowledge of anything, but they seem to be able to communicate quite effectively. Let us move down from the primates. Everyone knows about the birds and the bees, but even social bacteria organize effectively using chemical signals.

Myxococcus xanthus are cooperative hunters. They swarm over prey and digest them. When starving, they aggregate and form a fruiting body, much like the cellular slime molds. Other bacteria use chemical signals to turn on bioluminescence, to form biofilms, and to turn on virulence.[4] This is all done without common knowledge or recursive mind reading—indeed, *without minds.*

The second reason to doubt that common knowledge is the basis of communication is that human beings themselves do not seem to be able to measure up. When it comes to knowing about knowing about knowing, or reasoning about reasoning about reasoning, quite a lot of experimental evidence shows that humans seem capable of going only a few levels up the ladder. This is one of the striking findings of behavioral game theory that challenge the foundations of the classical approach.

I think that Tomasello and I are in agreement that common knowledge is too strong an assumption for humans. Instead, he calls upon "common ground," which is a much more modest requirement. Common ground is stated in terms of mutual belief. In the first place, the beliefs need not be true. But more crucially, common ground—to the best of my understanding—only goes up one level in the hierarchy of shared beliefs. Humans, certainly, are capable of this.

Pure common interest between sender and receiver is favorable to communication, but if it were necessary there would be much less communication in the world than there is. If we look beyond common interest, we find cases of mixed interests leading to partial information transfer, and even cases of outright deception.

Outright deceptive signaling has struck some as impossible, but examples are not so hard to come by. For instance, when a female firefly of the genus *Photuris* observes a male of the genus *Photinus*, she may mimic the female signals of the male's species, lure him in, and eat him. She gets not only a nice meal, but also some useful protective chemicals that she cannot get in any other way. One species, *Photuris versicolor*, is a remarkably accomplished mimic, capable of sending the appropriate flash patterns of eleven *Photinus* species.

How can this pattern of deception persist? The *Photinus* species have their signaling systems in place, and encounters with *Photuris* are not sufficiently frequent to destroy it. It is not, then, a good scientific decision to make common interest a basic assumption of signaling theory.

I suggest that we move from the high rationality approach of classical game theory to a low rationality approach through adaptive dynamics. I have in mind two varieties of adaptive dynamics: evolution and reinforcement learning. These operate on different time scales, but they are not really so different. They are both varieties of trial-and-error learning. For evolution, the first formal model is replicator dynamics. Payoffs from interactions are measured in terms of Darwinian fitness—that is, in terms of how they translate to reproductive success. Bigger payoffs lead to a greater share of the population in the next generation. In the case of learning, I would like to focus on basic reinforcement learning.

Let us start with the simplest case of common interest without common knowledge. Nature flips a fair coin to pick one of two states. The sender observes the state and sends one of two signals. The receiver observes the signal and picks one of two acts. One act is "right" for each state, in that the sender and receiver each get a payoff of one if that act is done in that state, and each get a payoff of zero otherwise. In this situation, it has been shown that both evolution[5] and reinforcement learning[6] arrive at perfect signaling.

If we move from common interests to mixed interests, we now typically can be led (by either evolution or learning) to an equilibrium in which the sender transmits some information and conceals some. Information transmission without pure common interest occurs naturally in many contexts.

I would also consider low-rationality (and no-rationality) models of other phenomena that Tomasello discusses. One can have teamwork without team reasoning. I do not think that teamwork is a special attribute of humans, or that it necessarily requires human capabilities. Humans may well be more cooperative than chimpanzees—I leave it to the experts to judge—but we are far from being the most cooperative species on the planet. Meerkats, mole rats, many types of social insects, and even bacteria achieve high levels of cooperation. Cooperation often involves various kinds of feedback mechanisms, but recursive mind reading, higher-order intentions, and mutual belief are only relevant concepts in very special cases. I would not deny that these may be part of the story about how we do it, when we do it, but looking at cooperation in nature across a broad spectrum of organisms gives some useful perspective.

Elizabeth S. Spelke

MICHAEL TOMASELLO AIMS TO EXPLAIN THE unique cognitive accomplishments of our species. He asks why we humans, alone among the earth's living creatures, transform our surroundings by tools and agriculture; why we analyze and codify our physical and social environment through the creation and study of history, geography, and social institutions; why we enrich our social and material world through a panoply of endeavors including literature and music, theater and sports, mathematics and science.

His work begins with two general observations. First, humans are primates. Our basic capacities for perception, action, learning, memory, and emotion show deep similarities with those of other apes, and considerable similarity to those of monkeys and more remote relatives. These similarities underlie the development of a host of new enterprises in neuroscience, genetics, evolutionary biology, and psychology: fields in which scientists gain insight into our own species through studies of other animals. Tomasello, in particular, has discovered commonalities among humans and other apes in our understandings of people and objects.[1] These similarities shed light on both the nature and the evolution of capacities at the foundations of our social and material lives.

Second, we do some bizarre things with our primate minds: humans engage in activities that no other animal contemplates. All animals must locate and identify food, for example, but only humans cultivate, herd, and cook. All animals must find their way to significant places in their environment, but only humans navigate by maps and ponder the geometrical structure of the universe far beyond any place to which they could travel. Although many animals are sensitive to numerosity, only humans have a productive system of natural number concepts, organized around an iterative counting procedure. And while many animals must engage with other members of their own species in order to reproduce, raise their young, and organize their territory and its resources, only humans form complex social organizations such as schools, economies, factories, and armies. What sets humans on the paths that lead to these dramatic accomplishments?

To address this question, Tomasello and others have undertaken a threefold comparative approach to the study of human cognition. First, he and other students of animal cognition compare the cognitive capacities of different animal species, probing both for abilities and propensities that are widespread across animals and for those that are unique to primates, apes, or humans. Second, he and other students of human development compare the cognitive capacities of children of different ages, asking what capacities emerge earliest in development and what further achievements they allow. Tomasello's developmental research, in particular, illuminates a set of abilities and propensities that emerge at the start of the second year of life, remain present and functional at all later ages, and guide the development of a host of uniquely human cognitive achievements. Third, he and other linguists and anthropologists compare the cognitive achievements of children and adults in different cultures, so as to distinguish abilities and propensities that are universal across humans from those that depend on our cultural heritage and circumstances.

The earliest comparative approaches to the human mind were heavily criticized, in the last century, for positing a linear ordering from lower to higher animals, from simpler to more complex cognitive stages in humans, and from primitive to advanced cultures. But it is not clear that a linear model of change cannot work: phylogenesis, ontogenesis, and cultural development are rich and variegated. Tomasello and other contemporary investigators use comparative approaches precisely because human cognition is so complex. To make progress in understanding it, we must carve cognition at its joints, breaking high-level capacities into parts whose properties and interactions can be described and manipulated. Moreover, we must distinguish between the abilities that truly stand at the foundations of humans' distinctive cognitive capacities and the further abilities that these foundations support. Contemporary cognitive scientists use comparisons across species, ages, and human groups to find both the evolutionarily ancient foundational capacities we share with other species and the capacities that distinguish us as a species, that arise early in human development, and that show the greatest invariance across human cultures.

These threefold comparisons cast doubt on a number of venerable ideas about the sources of human uniqueness. For example, one idea places the capacity for tool use at the foundations of human cognitive achievements. Tomasello's studies of chimpanzees and children reveal, however, that while tool use is an important indication of our distinctive capacities, it is not their source. Distinctively human patterns of tool use arise only after the emergence of uniquely human forms of communication.[2] A second idea views humans as "the symbolic species"[3] that naturally extends its cognitive capacities by means of maps, pictures, writing systems, and other symbols. But research in developmental psychology suggests that children only begin to understand such symbols in the third year of life,[4] long after the uniquely human developments that Tomasello describes in these chapters. A third idea focuses on the capacity for abstraction: humans are uniquely able to form and manipulate abstract concepts that enable, for example, the development of mathematics. Research in animal cognition, however, has found abstract numerical representations in a wide range of nonhuman animals.[5] And both developmental and cross-cultural studies further undermine the abstract-thought thesis by revealing that some of our most important abstract concepts, such as the system of natural numbers, emerge after, and depend upon, the acquisition of language and verbal counting.[6]

So what are the innate differences between humans and other animals that give rise to humans' unique accomplishments? Tomasello's answer has changed in some ways over time,[7] a sign of his openness and productivity. The elegant experiments that he and his students have conducted have taught us that a number of perfectly sensible ideas about human nature turn out to be wrong. Despite these changes, however, a common theme runs through his work: the key to our unique nature resides in our distinctive social relationships. In these pages, Tomasello argues that the unique features of human cognition are rooted in an evolved, species specific capacity and motivation for *shared intentionality* that gives rise to distinctive kinds of communication and joint action. Humans, on this view, are naturally driven to cooperate with one another and to share information, tasks, and goals. From this capacity spring all of our other distinctive achievements, from tool use to mathematics to symbols.

I think Tomasello's hypothesis has a chance of being right, but at least one competitor is alive and well: the view that human language is the source of our unique cognitive achievements. This view gains support, in part, from research that begins with younger human infants. Like Tomasello, I probe for the sources of human uniqueness by comparing cognitive capacities across species, ages, and cultures. I focus, however, on cognitive capacities manifest in the first months of human life, asking whether they exist in other animals, and what happens to them over the course of human development in our own and other cultures.

To summarize a few decades of experiments, I believe there is evidence for at least five cognitive systems in young infants: what I call systems of *core knowledge*.[8] These are systems for representing and reasoning about (1) inanimate, material objects and their motions, (2) intentional agents and their goal-directed actions, (3) places in the navigable environment and their geometric relations to one another (4) sets of objects or events and their numerical relationships of ordering and arithmetic, and (5) social partners who engage with the infant in reciprocal interactions. Each of these cognitive systems emerges early in infancy (in some cases, at birth) and remains present, and essentially unchanged, as children grow. Thus, the systems are universal across our species, despite the many differences in the practices and belief systems of people in different cultural groups. Most important, these core knowledge systems are relatively separate from one another and limited in their domains of application. Children and adults bring them together, and overcome their signature limits, when they learn and practice later-developing, culturally variable, and uniquely human cognitive skills. These later developments, in turn, are related to children's acquisition of a natural language.

The core system for representing objects illustrates these findings. When infants in the first six months of life are presented with objects under controlled conditions, their spontaneous reactions of looking or reaching to the objects shed light on both the nature and the limits of their object representations. These experiments reveal that even newborn infants share some mature human capacities for representing objects: when tested under the right conditions, infants keep track of visible objects, infer what hidden parts of objects look like, and even represent objects that have been moved fully out of view.[9]

Nevertheless, infants' object representations show some quirky limitations. As adults, we can single out many different kinds of things, including cups, doorknobs, sand piles, trees, and towers made of blocks. Presented with each of these kinds of entities, however, infants represent only those that are internally cohesive and separately movable: the cups but not the doorknobs, sand piles, or block towers.[10] Infants also cannot keep track of more than three objects at any given time.[11] Most important, young infants fail to represent objects as members of kinds, with dedicated functions. These limits serve as signatures that can indicate whether the core system continues to exist in adults in our culture and others, whether it is shared by other animals, and whether children and adults draw on this core system when they attempt to master new ways of thinking about the physical world. The answer to all of these questions is yes.

When adults follow visible objects about which we have little culture-specific knowledge, we show the same abilities that infants have, with the same signature limits.[12] Members of distant cultures perform the same object-representation tasks with similar results.[13] When older children begin to acquire names for objects, master counting, and reason about the mechanical interactions among objects, core notions of objects leave their imprint on each of these developments.[14] Infants' object representations therefore figure in the development of a host of uniquely human abilities.

Nevertheless, core object representations are not unique to humans. Semi-free-ranging rhesus monkeys form the same object representations, with the same signature limits as infants.[15] Research reveals common properties of these representations even in animals that are considerably more distant from humans, such as birds.[16] Core capacities for object representation therefore do not explain our unique human capacities for reasoning about the physical world: they account neither for our propensity for tool use nor for our capacity for formal science.

Even though infants' systems of core knowledge are not unique to humans, studies of these systems provide valuable tools for examining human cognition. Because our unique cognitive abilities build on core-knowledge systems that are shared by other animals, we can probe the development of these systems by studying other species, using the diverse, powerful techniques of neuroscience, genetics, behavioral ecology, and controlled rearing.[17] Moreover, we can study developing children and ask what distinguishes their uniquely human ways of representing objects from the core representations of younger infants and other animals.

Both human infants and adult monkeys can learn about the functional properties of specific objects—though slowly, in a piecemeal fashion.[18] Neither young infants nor adult monkeys, however, are rapid and flexible tool learners. In their second year of life, human children, and only human children, start putting together information about objects and actions productively. They come to view virtually every new object they see both as a mechanical body with a particular kind of form and as a potentially useful *tool* with a particular, dedicated function in the service of goal-directed action.

What accounts for this explosion of learning about artifacts? Recent research suggests children's artifact concepts have two sources: the core system of object representation just described and a second core system for representing agents and their goal-directed actions. From a very early age, human infants represent the actions of other people and animals as directed toward goals and as similar in purpose and form to the actions of the self.[19] Like core representations of objects, core representations of goal-directed actions are very similar in human infants and in nonhuman primates.[20] In their second year of life, however, human children start putting together information about objects and actions productively. The productive joining of object representations and action representations appears to be unique to our species, even though the core systems on which it builds are not.

What sparks the prolific development of tool concepts in children? Research from a number of sources suggests that this development depends in some way on children's learning of words as names for kinds of objects. This new linguistic format functions to join core representations. For instance, when infants learn their first object names, they put together information about object form and object function that previously was represented quite separately.[21] Object names also focus infants' attention on object categories: on what two different hammers or cups have in common.[22] Even adults who imagine tool objects and their associated functions, such as hammering, activate secondary language areas of the brain: areas that may orchestrate representations of object structure and function.[23] Language—a combinatorial system par excellence—serves to combine representations of objects and actions rapidly, flexibly, and productively, giving rise to our prolific capacity to learn about and use tools.

I have focused on the development of tool use, but other distinctively human capacities appear to undergo a similar pattern of development. For example, human infants and other animals have a core system for representing numerosity, with its own distinctive limits—in particular, it is approximate and non-recursive—that preclude a full representation of natural numbers. Natural-number concepts emerge in the fourth or fifth year of life, when children learn number words, natural language quantification, and verbal counting: learning that leads them to combine their core representations of numerosity with their core representations of small numbers of objects.[24] As a further example, human infants and other animals have core systems for representing the shapes of two-dimensional forms and the shape of the large-scale, surrounding surface layout, but these systems are distinct and largely unrelated. In the third year, children begin to relate these systems through the use of language and thereby gain the ability to navigate by geometric maps.[25] Three hallmarks of uniquely human cognition—tool use, natural numbers, and geometry—appear to be consequences of a uniquely human combinatorial capacity that is linked to natural language.

When one considers these findings in relation to the research described by Tomasello, a natural question emerges: How does the human capacity for natural language, with the combinatorial power that it affords, relate to the human capacity for shared intentionality? Tomasello does not deny that language is an important, even crucial, cognitive tool for humans. He argues, however, that the acquisition of language itself requires an explanation, and our foundational capacity for shared intentionality provides it.[26] Language acquisition, in Tomasello's view, is not the product of a genetically specified language faculty. Instead, it is constructed by children over the course of their interactions with other people as they, and their social partners, focus jointly on objects and on one another. On this view, natural language is the product, not the source, of our uniquely human ways of cooperating and communicating.

It is possible, however, that the causal arrow points in the opposite direction. Uniquely human forms of shared intentionality may depend upon our uniquely human capacity for combining core representations productively. On this rival view, there are no uniquely human core systems in any substantive domain of cognition, including the domain of social reasoning. Only language has uniquely human core foundations, and it serves to represent and express concepts within and across all knowledge domains. Humans' unique ability to put together distinct core representations rapidly, productively, and flexibly may reside, therefore, in our innate faculty for language.

These two accounts—language as a product of uniquely human social interactions versus language as the source of those interactions—can best be distinguished by probing the origins of shared intentionality, through studies of younger infants. Young human infants are social in many ways. At birth, infants discriminate between different human people and attend to their direction of gaze.[27] Newborn infants also are sensitive to some correspondences between their own actions and the actions of other people, and they use this sensitivity to engage in an early form of imitation: they produce movements that are related to the movements they see.[28]

Crucially, however, none of these social capacities is unique to humans. Nonhuman primates are sensitive to faces even in the absence of prior visual experience,[29] they follow gaze to objects,[30] and they detect correspondences between their own actions and those of others even as newborns, engaging in patterns of imitation that are strikingly like those of newborn humans.[31] These findings suggest that our core sociality—our interest in other people and our abilities to perceive and engage with them—is not unique to our species.

Moreover, the core system for understanding other people as social partners appears to be quite disconnected from the core system for understanding other people as goal-directed agents. Although young infants (and other animals) view other members of their species both as agents who act on objects and as partners who share their mental states, there is no evidence that they combine these notions flexibly or productively. Failures to combine representations of actors and social partners could explain why nonhuman animals and young infants do not treat other people as communicators and collaborators, whose goal-directed actions can be coordinated with their own through patterns of cooperation and shared attention.

As Tomasello's research beautifully reveals, shared intentionality—the triadic relationship of the self both to a social partner and to the objects of goal-directed actions—emerges around the beginning of the second year of life. From that time onward, children point in order to convey information, they discern other people's intentions from the direction of their gaze, they infer other people's states of knowledge from their past actions and perceptions, and they help others to achieve their goals. Shared intentionality may well be an integrated system at these ages, but is it the keystone of human uniqueness, or is this communicative system constructed—like tools, natural numbers, and symbolic maps—from a combinatorial capacity that is more fundamental still, and that operates by conjoining preexisting core systems of knowledge through the use of language?

Existing research does not decisively answer this question, but some findings favor the latter view. On this view, we might expect shared intentionality to emerge piecemeal, as language is gradually learned and representations gradually combined, rather than as one innate, integrated whole. This appears to be the case. At ten months of age, when infants are in the process of developing understanding of communicative actions such as pointing, and of states of social attention such as mutual gaze, these developments are not closely related: a child may master one of these domains while making little progress in the other.[32] Moreover, ten-month-old infants reliably follow a person's gaze to the object at which she is looking and look at an object to which she is reaching, but they fail to connect these two abilities so as to predict that a person will reach for the object to which she looks.[33] These findings suggest that young infants fail to integrate their understanding of people as actors with their understanding of people as perceivers who share their own experiences of the surrounding world. Therefore, shared intentionality emerges in pieces, as one might predict if the child's developing language served to connect her otherwise disparate cognitive capacities.

How might these two conceptions be integrated to form the triadic relationship between an infant, her social partner, and the objects that both perceive and act upon? Children may construct the triangle of shared intentionality at the end of the first year, by harnessing the power of natural language. Natural-language expressions may serve as the critical link between agents, social partners, and objects, because words have two faces: (1) they refer to objects and (2) they are a medium of social exchange. Just as children may become tool users by using natural-language expressions to combine productively their core representations of objects and agents, they may become intentional communicators and cooperators by using such expressions to combine productively their core concepts of agents and social partners. Distinctively human forms of communication and cooperation may depend on uniquely human combinatorial capacities.

I have focused my remarks on two different attempts to explain humans' unique cognitive capacities: Tomasello's notion of an innate, species-specific capacity for shared intentionality, and the notion of an innate, species-specific combinatorial capacity expressed in natural language. At this time, we cannot know whether either of these accounts is correct. Nevertheless, I believe that Tomasello's findings have focused current thinking in a fruitful direction, and his methods provide a model for advancing our understanding.

To make further progress, however, investigators need to harness the kind of ingenuity Tomasello has shown in extracting insights from observations of one-, two-, or three-year-old children, and probe the sociality of younger infants, both human and nonhuman. As in the case of object representation, a panoply of methods, from neurophysiology to controlled-rearing studies, can be assembled to explore the earliest emerging capacities for social knowledge.[34] Armed with a better understanding of humans' earliest-developing social knowledge, investigators can then explore the key developmental events that lead to the emergence, in the second year, of the remarkable patterns of communication and cooperation that Tomasello's work reveals. Experiments that enhance young infants' social or linguistic experience, and then assess the cognitive consequences of this enhancement, may be especially illuminating for this purpose.[35]

Whatever the outcome of these studies, Tomasello's work gives us reason to believe that the next decade of research exploring the minds and actions of infants will be as fruitful as the last. The fundamental questions of human nature and human knowledge, questions that have been outstanding for millennia, are beginning to yield answers, and I believe will now particularly bear fruit through comparative work with the youngest members of our species.

Notes

Introduction

[1] Tomasello, M., Kruger, A., and Ratner, H. 1993. "Cultural learning." *Behavioral and Brain Sciences* 16(3): 495–511.

[2] Richerson, P. and Boyd, R. 2006. *Not by genes alone: How culture transformed human evolution.* Chicago: University of Chicago Press.

[3] Searle, J. R. 1995. *The Construction of Social Reality.* New York: Free Press.

[4] Bratman, M. 1992. "Shared co-operative activity." *Philosophical Review* 101(2): 327–341. Gilbert, M.

1989. *On Social Facts.* Princeton: Princeton University Press. Searle, J. R. 1995. *The Construction of Social Reality.* Tuomela, R. 2007. *The Philosophy of Sociality: The Shared Point of View.* Oxford: Oxford University Press.

[5] Tomasello, M.; Carpenter, M.; Call, J.; Behne, T.; and Moll, H. 2005. "Understanding and sharing intentions: The origins of cultural cognition." *Behavioral and Brain Sciences* 28(5): 675–691.

[6] Tomasello, M. 1999. *The Cultural Origins of Human Cognition.* Cambridge, Mass.: Harvard University Press.

[7] Herrmann, E.; Call, J.; Lloreda, M.; Hare, B.; and Tomasello, M. 2007. "Humans have evolved specialized skills of social cognition: The cultural intelligence hypothesis." *Science* 317(5843): 1360–1366.

Chapter 1

[1] Warneken, F. and Tomasello, M. In press. "Roots of human altruism." *British Journal of Psychology.*

[2] Warneken, F. and Tomasello, M. 2006. "Altruis-

tic helping in human infants and young chimpanzees." *Science* 311(5765): 1301–1303. Warneken, F., and Tomasello, M. 2007. "Helping and cooperation at 14 months of age." *Infancy* 11: 271–294. Videos of this helping behavior are available at bostonreview.net/whywecooperate.

[3] Warneken, F.; Hare, B.; Melis, A.; Hanus, D.; and Tomasello, M. 2007. "Spontaneous altruism by chimpanzees and young children." *PLOS Biology* 5(7): e184.

[4] Warneken, F. and Tomasello, M. 2008. "Extrinsic rewards undermine altruistic tendencies in 20-month-olds." *Developmental Psychology* 44(6): 1785–1788.

[5] Warneken, F. and Tomasello, M. 2006. "Altruistic helping in human infants and young chimpanzees."

[6] Warneken, F., et al. 2007. "Spontaneous altruism by chimpanzees and young children."

[7] Callaghan, T., pending.

[8] Vaish, A.; Carpenter, M.; and Tomasello, M. In press. "Sympathy, affective perspective-taking, and

prosocial behavior in young children." *Developmental Psychology.*

[9] Kuhlmeier, V.; Wynne, K.; and Bloom, P. 2003. "Attribution of dispositional states by 12-month-olds." *Psychological Science* 14(5): 402–408.

[10] Liszkowski, U.; Carpenter, M.; Striano, T.; and Tomasello, M. 2006. "12- and 18-month-olds point to provide information for others." *Journal of Cognition and Development* 7(2): 173–187.

[11] Liszkowski, U.; Carpenter, M.; and Tomasello, M. 2008. "Twelve-month-olds communicate helpfully and appropriately for knowledgeable and ignorant partners." *Cognition* 108(3): 732–739.

[12] Leavens, D. A.; Hopkins, W. D.; and Bard, K. A. 2005. "Understanding the point of chimpanzee pointing: Epigenesis and ecological validity." *Current Directions in Psychological Science* 14(4): 185–189.

[13] Call, J. and Tomasello, M. 1994. "The production and comprehension of referential pointing by orangutans." *Journal of Comparative Psychology* 108(4): 307–317.

[14] Bullinger, A.; Kaminski, J.; Zimmerman, F.; and Tomasello, M. Submitted. "Different social motives in the gestural communication of chimpanzees and human children."

[15] Tomasello, M. 2006. "Why don't apes point?" In N. Enfield & S. Levinson (Eds.), *Roots of Human Sociality*. New York: Wenner-Grenn.

[16] Behne, T.; Carpenter, M.; and Tomasello, M. 2005. "One-year-olds comprehend the communicative intentions behind gestures in a hiding game." *Developmental Science* 8(6): 492–499.

[17] Two leading research teams agree. "Listeners acquire information from signalers who do not, in the human sense, intend to provide it," write Robert M. Seyfarth and Dorothy L. Cheney in "Signalers and receivers in animal communication." *Annual Review of Psychology* 54: 145–173. Klaus Zuberbühler writes, "Nonhuman primates vocalize in response to important events, irrespective of how potential recipients may view the situation." In "The phylogenetic roots of language: Evidence from primate communication

and cognition." *Current Directions in Psychological Science* 14(3): 126–130.

[18] Grosse, G.; Moll, H.; and Tomasello, M. Submitted. "21-Month-Olds Understand the Co-operative Logic of Requests."

[19] Silk, J. B.; Brosnan, S. F.; Vonk, J.; Henrich, J.; Povinelli, D. J.; Richardson, A. S.; Lambeth, S. P.; Mascaro, J.; and Schapiro, S. J. 2005. "Chimpanzees are indifferent to the welfare of unrelated group members." *Nature* 437: 1357–1359. Jensen, K.; Hare, B.; Call, J.; and Tomasello, M. 2006. "What's in it for me? Self-regard precludes altruism and spite in chimpanzees." *Proceedings of the Royal Society of London, Series B - Biological Sciences* 273(1589): 1013–1021.

[20] Fehr, E.; Bernhard, H.; and Rockenbach; B. 2008. "Egalitarianism in young children." *Nature* 454: 1079–1083. Brownell, C.; Svetlova, M.; and Nichols, S. 2009. "To share or not to share: When do toddlers respond to another's need?" *Infancy* 14(1): 117–130.

21 Melis, A.; Hare, B.; and Tomasello, M. 2006. "Engineering cooperation in chimpanzees: tolerance constraints on cooperation." *Animal Behaviour* 72(2): 275–286.

22 Muller, M. and Mitani, J. 2005. "Conflict and cooperation in wild chimpanzees." *Advances in the Study of Behavior* 35: 275–331.

23 de Waal, F. B. M. 1989. "Food sharing and reciprocal obligations among chimpanzees." *Journal of Human Evolution* 18(5): 433–459.

24 Ueno, A. and Matsuzawa, T. 2004. "Food transfer between chimpanzee mothers and their infants." *Primates* 45 (4): 231 239.

25 Olson, K. R. and Spelke, E. S. 2008. "Foundations of cooperation in preschool children." *Cognition* 108(1): 222–231.

26 Vaish, A.; Carpenter, M.; and Tomasello, M. Submitted. "Children help others based on moral judgments about them."

27 Muller, M., and Mitani, J. 2005. "Conflict and cooperation in wild chimpanzees." Melis, A.; Hare, B.;

and Tomasello, M. 2008. "Do chimpanzees reciprocate received favours?" *Animal Behaviour* 76(3): 951–962.

[28] Dweck, C. 2000. *Self-Theories: Their Role in Motivation, Personalsty and Development.* Philadelphia: Psychology Press.

[29] Brosnan, S. F. and de Waal, F. B. M. 2003. "Monkeys reject unequal pay." *Nature* 425: 297–299.

[30] Brosnan, S. F.; Schiff, H. C.; and de Waal, F. 2005. "Tolerance for inequity may increase with social closeness in chimpanzees." *Proceedings of the Royal Society B* 272(1560): 253–258.

[31] Bräuer, J.; Call, J.; and Tomasello, M. 2006. "Are apes really inequity averse?" *Proceedings of the Royal Society B* 273(1605): 3123–3128.

[32] Jensen, K.; Call, J.; and Tomasello, M. 2007. "Chimpanzees are rational maximizers in an ultimatum game." *Science* 318(5847): 107–109.

[33] Great apes discourage antisocial behavior, but without social norms—they retaliate against others who harm them (or their children) and avoid non-coop-

erators when choosing partners.

34 Kalish, C. W. 2006. "Integrating normative and psychological knowledge: What should we be thinking about?" *Journal of Cognition and Culture* 6: 161–178.

35 Piaget, J. 1935. *The moral judgment of the child.* New York: Free Press.

36 Rakoczy, H.; Warneken, F.; and Tomasello, M. 2008. "The sources of normativity: Young children's awareness of the normative structure of games." *Developmental Psychology* 44(3): 875–881. See also Rakoczy, H.; Brosche, N.; Warneken, F.; and Tomasello, M. In press. "Young children's understanding of the context relativity of normative rules." *British Journal of Developmental Psychology.*

37 Though the child may not recognize the arbitrariness, see Kalish, 2006, on this possibility with other types of conventionality.

38 Nagel, T. 1970. *The possibility of altruism.* Princeton, N.J.: Princeton University Press.

39 Tomasello, M. and Rakoczy, H. 2003. "What

makes human cognition unique? From individual to shared to collective intentionality." *Mind and Language* 18(2): 121–147.

[40] Moral norms have a "natural" component as well. See Nichols, S. 2004. *Sentimental Rules: On the Natural Foundations of Moral Judgment*. New York: Oxford University Press.

[41] See Durham, W. 1992. *Coevolution: Genes, Culture and Human Diversity*. Palo Alto, Calif.: Stanford University Press.

Chapter 2

[1] Searle, J. R. 1995. *The Construction of Social Reality*.

[2] For a compelling argument in this direction, see Sterelny, K. 2008. *Nicod Lectures*: http://www.institutnicod.org/lectures2008_outline.htm.

[3] Bratman, M. 1992. "Shared co-operative activity." Gilbert, M. 1989. *On Social Facts*.

[4] Clark, H. 1996. *Uses of Language*. Cambridge: Cambridge University Press.

[5] Boesch, C. 2005. "Joint cooperative hunting among wild chimpanzees: Taking natural observations seriously." *Behavioral and Brain Sciences* 28(5): 692–693.

[6] Tuomela, R. 2007. *The Philosophy of Sociality: The Shared Point of View.*

[7] Warneken, F. and Tomasello, M. 2006. "Altruistic helping in human infants and young chimpanzees." Warneken, F., et al. 2007 "Spontaneous altruism by chimpanzees and young children." Videos of this collaborative behavior are available at bostonreview.net/whywecooperate.

[8] Hammann, K., et al. (ongoing).

[9] Gräfenhein, M.; Behne, T.; Carpenter, M.; and Tomasello, M. In press. "Young children's understanding of joint commitments to cooperate." *Developmental Psychology.*

[10] Carpenter, M.; Tomasello, M.; and Striano, T. 2005. "Role reversal imitation in 12 and 18 month olds and children with autism." *Infancy* 8(3): 253–278.

[11] Tomasello, M. and Carpenter, M. 2005. "The emergence of social cognition in three young chimpanzees." *Monographs of the Society for Research in Child Development* 70, no. 279.

[12] Moll, H., and Tomasello, M. 2007. "Cooperation and human cognition: The Vygotskian intelligence hypothesis." *Philosophical Transactions of the Royal Society B* 362(1480): 639–648.

[13] Moll, H.; Koring, C.; Carpenter, M.; and Tomasello, M. 2006. "Infants determine others' focus of attention by pragmatics and exclusion." *Journal of Cognition & Development* 7(3): 411–430.

[14] Tomasello, M., and Carpenter, M. 2005. "The emergence of social cognition in three young chimpanzees."

[15] Call, J., and Tomasello, M. 2008. "Does the chimpanzee have a theory of mind: 30 years later." *Trends in Cognitive Science* 12(5): 187–92.

[16] Tomasello, M. 2008. *Origins of Human Communication*.

[17] Grice, P. 1975. "Logic and conversation." In Cole,

P. and Morgan, J., (Eds.), *Syntax and Semantics: Vol. 3. Speech Acts.* New York: Academic Press.

[18] Wittgenstein, L. 1953. *Philosophical Investigations.* Oxford: Basil Blackwell.

[19] Skyrms, B. 2004. *The Stag Hunt and the Evolution of Social Structure.* Cambridge, U.K.: Cambridge U. Press.

[20] See also Sterelny, K. 2008. *Nicod Lectures*, available at http://www.institutnicod.org/lectures2008_outline.htm.

[21] Tomasello, M.; Hare, B.; Lehmann, H.; and Call, J. 2007. "Reliance on head versus eyes in the gaze following of great apes and human infants: The cooperative eye hypothesis." *Journal of Human Evolution* 52(3): 314–320.

[22] Boesch, C. 2005. "Joint cooperative hunting among wild chimpanzees: Taking natural observations seriously."

[23] Gilby, I. C. 2006. "Meat sharing among the Gombe chimpanzees: Harassment and reciprocal exchange." *Animal Behaviour* 71(4): 953–963.

[24] Hare, B.; Melis, A.; Woods, V.; Hastings, S.; and Wrangham, R. 2007. "Tolerance allows bonobos to outperform chimpanzees in a cooperative task." *Current Biology* 17(7): 619–623.

[25] Hare, B. and Tomasello, M. 2005. "Human-like social skills in dogs?" *Trends in Cognitive Science* 9(9): 439–444.

[26] Hrdy, S. 2009. *Mothers and others.* Cambridge, Mass.: Harvard University Press.

[27] Melis, A.; Hare, B.; and Tomasello, M. 2006. "Chimpanzees recruit the best collaborators." *Science* 311(5765): 1297–1300.

[28] Jensen, K.; Call, J.; and Tomasello, M. 2007. "Chimpanzees are vengeful but not spiteful." *Proceedings of the National Academy of Sciences* 104(32): 13046-13050.

[29] Knight, J. 1992. *Institutions and social conflict.* Cambridge, U.K.: Cambridge University Press.

[30] Richerson, P. and Boyd, R. 2006. *Not by genes alone: How culture transformed human evolution.*

[31] Kinzler, K. D.; Dupoux, E.; and Spelke, E. S. 2007.

"The native language of social cognition." *Proceedings of the National Academy of Sciences* 104(30): 12577-12580.

[32] Durham, W. 1992. *Coevolution: Genes, Culture and Human Diversity.* Palo Alto, Calif.: Stanford University Press.

[33] I have attempted to tell it in my recent book *Origins of Human Communication.* Tomasello, M. 2008.

[34] Rakoczy, H. and Tomasello, M. 2007. "The ontogeny of social ontology: Steps to shared intentionality and status functions." In Tsohatzidis, S. (Ed.), *Intentional Acts and Institutional Facts: Essays on John Searle's Social Ontology.* Berlin: Springer Verlag.

[35] Wyman, E., et al. (in press).

Chapter 3

[1] Diamond, J. 1997. *Guns, Germs, and Steel: The Fates of Human Societies.* New York: W.W. Norton.

Silk

[1] Richerson, P. J., and Boyd, R. 2006. *Not by Genes*

Alone.

[2] Fehr, E., and Fischbacher, U. 2003. "The nature of human altruism." *Nature* 425: 785–791.

[3] Skyrms, B. 2004. *The Stag Hunt and Evolution of Social Structure.*

[4] Melis, A., et al. 2006. "Engineering cooperation in chimpanzees."

[5] Bronstein, J.L. 1994. "Our current understanding of mutualism." *Quarterly Review of Biology* 69(1): 31–51.

[6] Bergstrom, C. T., and Lachmann, M. 2003. "The Red King effect: evolutionary rates and division of surpluses in mutualisms." In Hammerstein, P. (Ed.), *Genetic and Cultural Evolution of Cooperation.* Cambridge, Mass.: MIT Press. Bronstein, J.L. 2003. "The scope for exploitation within mutualistic interactions." In Hammerstein, P. (Ed.), *Genetic and Cultural Evolution of Cooperation.*

[7] Jensen, K., et al. 2006. "What's in it for me?" Silk et al. 2005. "Chimpanzees are indifferent to the welfare of other group members." Vonk, J.; Brosnan, S. F.;

Silk, J. B.; Henrich, J.; Richardson, A. S.; Lambeth, S. P.; Schapiro, S. J.; and Povinelli, D.J. 2008. "Chimpanzees do not take advantage of very low cost opportunities to deliver food to unrelated group members." *Animal Behaviour* 75(5): 1757–1770.

[8] Whiten, A., and Byrne, R.W. 1997. *Machiavellian Intelligence II.* Oxford: Oxford University Press.

[9] Trivers, R. L. 1971. "The evolution of reciprocal altruism." *Quarterly Review of Biology* 46(1). 35–57. Axelrod, R., and Hamilton, W. D. 1981. "The evolution of cooperation." *Science* 211: 1390–1396.

[10] Silk, J. B.; Cheney, D. L.; and Seyfarth, R.M. 1999. "The structure of social relationships among female savannah baboons in Moremi Reserve, Botswana." *Behaviour* 136: 679–703, Silk, J. B., Alunann, J., and Alberts, S. C. 2006. "Social relationships among adult female baboons (*Papio cynocephalus*) I. Variation in the strength of social bonds." *Behavioral Ecology and Sociobiology* 61(2): 183–195.

[11] Frank, R., and Silk, J. B. In press. "Impatient traders or contingent reciprocators? Evidence for the ex-

tended time course of grooming exchanges in baboons." *Behaviour.*

[12] Silk, J. B.; Alberts, S. C.; and Altmann, J. 2006. "Social relationships among adult female baboons (*Papio cynocephalus*) II: Variation in the quality and stability of social bonds." *Behavioral Ecology and Sociobiology* 61(2): 197–204.

[13] Boyd, R. and Richerson, P. J. 1988. "The evolution of reciprocity in sizable groups." *Journal of Theoretical Biology* 132(3), 337–356.

[14] Fehr, E. and Fischbacher, U. 2003. "The nature of human altruism." Richerson, P. J., and Boyd, R. 2006. *Not by Genes Alone.*

[15] Mayr, U.; Harbaugh W. T.; and Tankersley, D. 2008. "Neuroeconomics of charitable giving and philanthropy." In Glimcher, P. W.; Camerer, C. F.; Fehr, E.; and Poldrack, R. A., (Eds.) *Neuroeconomics: Decision Making and the Brain.* Amsterdam: Elsevier.

Dweck

[1] See, e.g., Spelke, E.S. and Kinzler, K.D. 2007. "Core

knowledge." *Developmental Science* 10(1): 89–91.

[2] Saffran, J.R.; Aslin, R.N.; and Newport, E.L. 1996. "Statistical learning in 8-month-old infants." *Science* 274: 1926–1928.

[3] Johnson, S.; Dweck, C.S.; and Chen, F. 2007. "Evidence for infants' internal working models of attachment." *Psychological Science* 18(6): 501–502.

[4] Main, M., and George, C. 1985. "Responses of young abused and disadvantaged toddlers to distress in agemates." *Developmental Psychology* 21(3): 407–412.

[5] cf. Meltzoff, A.N. and Brooks, R. 2001. "'Like me' as a building block for understanding other minds: Bodily acts, attention, and intention." In Malle, B; Moses, L.; and Baldwin, D. (Eds.). *Intentions and intentionality: Foundations of social cognition.* Cambridge, Mass.: MIT Press.

[6] Hamlin, J.K.; Wynn, K.; and Bloom, P. 2007. "Social evaluation by preverbal infants." *Nature* 450: 557–559.

Skyrms

[1] Lewis has additional conditions, too. Unilateral deviation from a convention hurts others as well as oneself. But these details are not important here.

[2] Grice knew, of course, that the cooperative principle could be violated, even flouted, in conversation. Nevertheless the cooperative principle was taken as basic and the violations as depending on that basic usage.

[3] Lewis, however, does not bring players' intentions into the picture—and does not think that he has to.

[4] Taga, M. E. and Bassler, B. L. 2003. "Chemical Communication Among Bacteria." *Proceedings of the National Academy of Sciences of the USA* 100 (Suppl. 2): 14549–14554. Watnick, P. and Kolter, R. 2000. "Biofilm, City of Microbes." *Journal of Bacteriology* 182(10): 2675-2679.

[5] Hofbauer, J. and Huttegger, S. 2008. "Feasibility of Communication in Binary Signaling Games." *Journal of Theoretical Biology* 254(4): 843–849.

[6] Argiento, R.; Pemantle, R.; Skyrms, B.; and Volkov, S. 2009. "Learning to Signal: Analysis of a Micro-Level Reinforcement Model." *Stochastic Processes and their Applications* 119(2): 373–390.

Spelke
[1] Hare, B.; Call, J.; Agnetta, B.; and Tomasello, M. 2000. "Chimpanzees know what conspecifics do and do not see." *Animal Behaviour* 59(4): 771–785.

[2] Tomasello, M. 2008. *Origins of Human Communication.*

[3] Deacon, T. 1997. *The symbolic species: The co-evolution of language and the brain.* New York: W.W. Norton.

[4] DeLoache, J. S. 1995. "Early understanding and use of symbols." *Current Directions in Psychological Science* 4(4): 109–113.

[5] Dehaene, S. 1997. *The number sense: How the mind creates mathematics.* New York: Oxford University Press.

[6] Carey, S. 2009. *The origin of concepts.* New York:

Oxford University Press.

[7] Tomasello, M. and Call, J. 1997. *Primate cognition*. New York: Oxford University Press. Tomasello, M. 1999. *The Cultural Origins of Human Cognition*. Tomasello, M. 2008. *Origins of Human Communication*.

[8] Spelke, E. S. and Kinzler, K. D. 2007.

[9] For review see Baillargeon, R. 2004. "Infants' physical world." *Current Directions in Psychological Science* 13(3): 89–94.

[10] Spelke, E. S. 1990. "Principles of object perception." *Cognitive Science* 14(1): 29–56. Rosenberg, R., & Carey, S. 2006. "Infants' indexing of objects vs. non-cohesive entities." Poster presented at the Biennial meeting of the International Society for Infant Studies. Chiang, W. C., and Wynn, K. 1998. "Infants' representations of collections." *Infant Behavior and Development* 21(2): 341.

[11] For review see Feigenson, L.; Dehaene, S.; and Spelke, E. S. 2004. "Core systems of number." *Trends in Cognitive Sciences* 8(7): 307–314.

[12] Cheries, E. W.; Mitroff, S. R.; Wynn, K.; and Scholl, B. J. In press. "Do the same principles constrain persisting object representations in infant cognition and adult perception? The cases of continuity and cohesion." In Hood, B. and Santos, L. (Eds.). *The origins of object knowledge.* New York: Oxford University Press.

[13] Gordon, P. 2004. "Numerical Cognition Without Words: Evidence from Amazonia." *Science* 306(5695): 496–499.

[14] Markman, E. 1991. *Categorization and naming in children: Problems of induction.* Cambridge, Mass.: MIT Press. Carey, S. 2009. *The origin of concepts.*

[15] Hood, B. and Santos, L. (Eds.) In press. *The origins of object knowledge.* New York: Oxford University Press.

[16] Regolin, L. and Vallortigara, G. 1995. "Perception of partly occluded objects by young chicks." *Perception & Psychophysics* 57(7): 971–976.

[17] Chiandetti, C. and Vallortigara, G. 2008. "Is there an innate geometric module? Effects of experience

with angular geometric cues on spatial re-orientation based on the shape of the environment." *Animal Cognition* 11(1): 139–146.

[18] Hood, B. and Santos, L. (Eds.) In press. *The origins of object knowledge.*

[19] Woodward, A. L. 2005. "The infant origins of intentional understanding." In Kail, R.V. (Ed.) *Advances in Child Development and Behavior*, Volume 33. Oxford: Elsevier.

[20] Santos, L. R.; Hauser, M. D.; and Spelke, E. S. 2002. "The representation of different domains of knowledge in human and non-human primates: Artifactual and food kinds." In Bekoff, M.; Allen, C.; and Burghardt, G. (Eds.) *The Cognitive Animal*. Cambridge, Mass.: MIT Press.

[21] Xu, F. 2007. "Concept formation and language development: Count nouns and object kinds." In Gaskill, G. (Ed.). *Oxford Handbook of Psycholinguistics*. New York: Oxford University Press.

[22] Waxman, S. and Braun, I. 2005. "Consistent (but not variable) names as invitations to form object cat-

egories." *Cognition* 95(3): B59–68.

[23] Johnson-Frey, S. H.; Newman-Norlund, R.; & Grafton, S. T. 2005. "A distributed left hemisphere network active during planning of everyday tool use skills." *Cerebral Cortex* 15(6): 681–695.

[24] Carey, S. 2009. *The origin of concepts.* Spelke, E. S. 2000. "Core knowledge." *American Psychologist* 55(11): 1233–1243.

[25] Winkler-Rhoades, N.; Carey, S.; and Spelke, E. S. 2009. *Young children navigate by purely geometric maps.* Denver, CO: Society for Research in Child Development.

[26] Tomasello, M. and Call, J. 1997. *Primate cognition.* Tomasello, M. 1999. *The Cultural Origins of Human Cognition.* Tomasello, M. 2008. *Origins of Human Communication.*

[27] Farroni, T.; Pividori, D.; Simion, F.; Massaccesi, S.; and Johnson, M. H. 2004. "Gaze following in newborns." *Infancy* 5(1): 39–60.

[28] Meltzoff, A. N., and Moore, M. K. 1977. "Imitation of Facial and Manual Gestures by Human Neo-

nates." *Science* 198(4312): 75–78.

[29] Sugita, Y. 2008. "Face perception in monkeys reared with no exposure to faces." *Proceedings of the National Academy of Sciences (USA)* 105(1): 394–398.

[30] Tomasello, M.; Hare, B.; and Agnetta, B. 1999. "Chimpanzees follow gaze direction geometrically." *Animal Behaviour* 58(4): 769–777.

[31] Myowa-Yamakoshi, M.; Tomonaga, M.; Tanaka, M.; and Matsuzawa, T. 2004. "Imitation in neonatal chimpanzees (Pan troglodytes)." *Developmental Science* 7(4): 437–442.

[32] Brune, C. W. and Woodward, A. L. 2007. "Social cognition and social responsiveness in 10-month-old infants." *Journal of Cognition and Development* 8(2): 133–158.

[33] Phillips, A.; Wellman, H.; and Spelke, E. 2002. "Infants' ability to connect gaze and emotional expression as cues to intentional action." *Cognition* 85(1): 53–78.

[34] Sugita, Y. 2008. "Face perception in monkeys reared with no exposure to faces."

[35] Woodward, A. L. and Needham, A. (Eds.) 2008. *Learning and the infant mind.* Oxford: Oxford University Press.

ACKNOWLEDGMENTS

THIS BOOK IS A SLIGHTLY MODIFIED VERSION OF the Tanner Lectures delivered at Stanford University in the winter of 2008. Because I wanted to retain the more informal style characteristic of lectures, there are fewer academic citations than one might typically expect. In many places I have not given proper credit to other investigators, simply citing books or reviews (often my own) to cover everything in an area; in most cases, the proper citations are contained in the cited sources. The bias toward my own work reflects my primary goal in these lectures and this book: introducing people to the research on ape and human cooperation that my collaborators and I have been doing in recent years. I beg the reader's indulgence for the omissions and egocentricity. I would like to thank the Tanner Committee (especially Debra Satz and Michael Bratman), the commentators cum contributors (Carol Dweck, Joan Silk, Brian Skyrms, and Elizabeth Spelke), and the attendees for a very rewarding three days. I would also like to thank my collaborators at the Max Planck Institute for Evolutionary Anthropology, past and present, for their continuing inspiration and ideas. Of special importance for the work reported here are Brian Hare, Alicia Melis, Hannes Rakoczy, and Felix Warneken.

ABOUT THE CONTRIBUTORS

MICHAEL TOMASELLO, Co-Director of the Max Planck Institute for Evolutionary Anthropology in Leipzig, Germany, is author of *Primate Cognition, The Cultural Origins of Human Cognition*, and *Origins of Human Communication*, among others. In 2006 he was awarded the Jean-Nicod Prize for his contributions to philosophy and cognitive science.

CAROL S. DWECK, Lewis and Virginia Eaton Professor of Psychology at Stanford University, has won numerous prizes for her research in social development and her achievements in education. Her recent book is *Mindset*.

JOAN B. SILK is Professor of Anthropology at the University of California, Los Angeles and co-author of *How Humans Evolved*.

BRIAN SKYRMS, Professor of Logic and Philosophy of Science at the University of California, Irvine and Professor of Philosophy at Stanford University, is author of *The Stag Hunt and the Evolution of Social Structure*. He is a fellow of the American Academy of Arts and Sciences and the National Academy of Sciences.

ELIZABETH S. SPELKE, Marshall L. Berkman Professor of Psychology at Harvard University, is a Gugenheim fellow and the 2009 winner of the Jean-Nicod Prize.

BOSTON REVIEW BOOKS

Boston Review Books is an imprint of *Boston Review*, a bimonthly magazine of ideas. The book series, like the magazine, is animated by hope, committed to equality, and convinced that the imagination eludes political categories. Visit bostonreview.net for more information.

Africa's Turn?   EDWARD MIGUEL

Inventing American History   WILLIAM HOGELAND

After America's Midlife Crisis   MICHAEL GECAN